We Were So Young

We Were So Young

A COLLEGE BOY BECOMES A WWII ARMY FLIER

James Alter

Copyright © 2003 by James Alter.

Library of Congress Number: 2003093777
ISBN: Hardcover 1-4134-1390-0
Softcover 1-4134-1389-7

All rights reserved. No part of this book may be reproduced or transmitted in any form or by any means, electronic or mechanical, including photocopying, recording, or by any information storage and retrieval system, without permission in writing from the copyright owner.

This book was printed in the United States of America.

To order additional copies of this book, contact:
Xlibris Corporation
1-888-795-4274
www.Xlibris.com
Orders@Xlibris.com
19407

TO THOSE GUYS IN THE 780TH
WHO NEVER CAME HOME, NEVER HAD A FAMILY,
NEVER SAW ANOTHER SUNSET,
AND NEVER HAD A CHANCE TO WRITE
A MEMOIR OF WW II.

*We read our mail and counted up our missions—
In bombers named for girls, we burned
The cities we had learned about in school—
Till our lives wore out; our bodies lay among
The people we had killed and never seen* . . . .

From *Losses* by Randall Jarrell (1944)

CHAPTER 1

I was standing in my library looking for something, when I found something else I'd long forgotten.

It was a small device—a toggle switch on a green metal box with a red protective cover. The cover was lettered "Bomb Release" and was spring-loaded for quick opening.

This was a salvo switch, once mounted alongside the bomb control panel in a B-24 heavy bomber. As the squadron flew over the target, the bombardier in the lead plane, sighting through his bombsight, would release his bombs. Simultaneously, the bombardiers or navigators in the other aircraft, would push their toggle switches and salvo their loads to make a tight and effective bomb pattern.

I had pried this particular switch from the panel of a B-24 as we landed in Connecticut, following a long and harrowing flight from Italy. It was only a few weeks after the end of the war in Europe. I was sure this airplane would never fly again and would surely drop no more bombs.

* * *

Surrounded by pictures of my children and their children, I stood there in my pleasant apartment, sixty years removed from the war and B-24s and salvo switches. Could it really be sixty years? My image in the hall mirror assured me it could.

I hadn't thought much about World War II for a long time and I began to feel I was watching an old black and white movie with a very young me in the feature role.

How had I ever allowed myself to be shot at in a cold sky, four or five miles over Germany, and why had I kept doing it thirty-one times? Why had I joined the Air Corps in the first place? And why was I thinking about these questions after six decades? Was it really that little bomb release contrivance that triggered this rush of old images—the same way it used to trigger my 500-pound bombs?

So I sat down and thought about it some more.

* * *

I've never seen flak so terrible. It's everywhere at once. We're nearly over the target—a Silesian oil refinery we call Black Blechhammer. I'm the navigator, and I'm also the guy who will toggle out the bombs. It's my eleventh mission and I'm eleven times more frightened than I was on the first one.

There's a rattling kind of sound like hail on a tin roof, or the heavy raindrops that come with a sudden summer storm. These are pieces of steel from an exploding German 88 shell a few yards too far from us to cause any damage. Maybe the next one will be a few yards closer.

In spite of a thick undercast, we seem to be over the target. Why doesn't the lead bombardier do his job and drop his load? Well, maybe we're not directly over the target yet, but we sure as hell are directly over those German gunners. We know that they know that we won't deviate from our present altitude, direction, or airspeed. We are committed. We are sitting ducks. We are shitting ducks.

At last our leader drops his bombs and I salvo ours. The skies are filled with ugly black bursts, interspersed with burning airplanes and parachuting men. There is a malevolent symmetry here. Hundreds of our bombs fall on the city below from our invisible airplanes above, and the flak comes up like thunder from equally invisible guns below. We are the blind - killing and being killed by the blind.

CHAPTER 2

On Sunday, December 7th, 1941, I had just finished lunch with a friend in the men's dorm at Purdue University. We were sitting in his room, when a guy came running down the hall shouting, "The Japs are bombing Pearl Harbor, the Japs are bombing Pearl Harbor." Within seconds every radio in the dormitory had been turned on and an assortment of announcers were discussing, in calamitous tones, the few details then available. This sudden intrusion into our lives would be with us always. We would forever remember exactly what we were doing at that instant.

The next morning, things became more focused. We listened to President Roosevelt deliver his "Day of Infamy" speech to a hastily assembled joint session of Congress. Shortly afterwards, came the Congressional Declaration of War. As I stood looking down from my window on the quiet streets of West Lafayette, the somber sounds of the broadcast were matched by my own equally somber thoughts.

The campus buzzed with misinformation. We would all be in uniform in a week; the Japs would be bombing Indiana in a month; the university would be closed for the duration and we'd never graduate.

As draft-age kids—the peacetime draft was already well under way—we listened breathlessly to every mumble from our radios. Suddenly, public newscasts had become personal. There were thousands of us on this engineering school campus—all young, bright, and healthy. Many of us, including myself, were still in our teens. We were top-of-the-line cannon fodder. Our overactive imaginations, fed by a growing flood of wartime movies, created fanciful scenes of what we would soon be doing, none of which had much to do with chemistry, calculus, or thermodynamics.

The actions of our elders—the university masters—were similarly overwrought. Within a few days, for example, it was gravely announced in a burst of public spiritedness, that because of this brand new war, Christmas vacation—scheduled to begin in less than two weeks—would be cancelled. Or maybe they simply said that Christmas would be cancelled. The predictable outcry over this ill-considered decision had scarcely begun, when the cancellation itself was summarily cancelled.

The school fathers had wisely decided that they would rather not face 10,000 idle students for two unscheduled weeks. And just possibly, they might have considered that the faculty's vacation plans would also be spoiled. There was, naturally, no contingency plan in place.

There were other hasty directives, mostly withdrawn. The impact of Pearl Harbor and the resulting patriotic determination to do something—anything—colored everything we said and did. Suiting up for a big war begins slowly and demands a certain measure of time. Through those first wartime months, millions of ordinary Americans had to temporarily dampen their fervor. And millions of robust young men simply milled about waiting for distant decisions to be made about their futures. The major currency of the day was the idle chatter of the rumormongers.

* * *

America was still acting out its Great Depression role. The Dow-Jones was just over 100. A new automobile was $800. My summer job paid $12 for a six day week. A newspaper was two cents, a phone call five, a stamp three. Some of us may have been aware of what Hitler was doing to Europe, and fewer of us what Japan was doing to China. Most folks seemed relatively undisturbed about the world in general.

* * *

After the initial we're-having-a-war excitement had cooled, one of the things that occurred to many of us was our ROTC status. Purdue was a land grant school and Reserve Officer Training was required of all freshman and sophomores. The ROTC branch of service at Purdue was the U.S. Field Artillery, and many of us wondered if our destiny was to soon begin active duty with the cannoneers.

One afternoon each week, I would rush back to my room and change into uniform—olive-drab trousers, khaki shirt with tie, a brass-buttoned blouse, and a broad brown leather belt with a big, carefully polished buckle. Then came an hour or two of classes on whatever the Army thought was important for us to know.

Every so often, there would be a formal parade. This was always an impressive show—especially since the war had begun to stir our patriotic juices. A thousand of us would assemble on a huge field and march—American flags and guidons flying, trucks and cannon rolling, and uniformed VIPs reviewing. Most of us declared that we hated it. Most of us were lying.

The fun part of ROTC were the field maneuvers. We'd pile into Army 6X6 trucks, each pulling a cannon or a caisson, and hustle out to a farm somewhere. The guns were unhitched and we'd practice how to aim and load. (But never fire.) The cannon were mostly French 75s—literally the "Guns of August," dating back to well before WW I—

and only too typical of the 1942 level of American military preparedness. It was nice to be outside and away from the campus, and there was something manly about playing with such real, albeit obsolete, hardware. More useful to our future perhaps, were our lessons on how to double-clutch a large Army truck.

As our campus days slowly trickled away, we held aimless discussions on patriotism, liberty, and immortality. We listened to Bach, Brahms, and Benny Goodman on 78 rpm records. (A symphony could require a dozen records.) We spent rambling afternoons in the meadows along the Wabash River. We put away vast quantities of a local beer called Champagne Velvet.

We probably did not understand it at the time, but we were savoring these artifacts of civilian life for a reason.

* * *

There was, however, an unexpected bright spot in that bleak winter. During our nearly aborted Christmas holiday, I met Trudy at a party in Chicago, and for the first time in my life, I was in love. She was a light blonde—nearly platinum. She was finely formed and had an infectious laugh. I thought she was incredible. On New Years Eve we sat chastely in the den of her parents' apartment and talked forever. She was the most wonderful girl in my limited world. I felt that the planets, and maybe even the stars, were in a flawless alignment for my future. I believed that she would be the perfect girl to leave behind as I went off to fight a war.

My travel arrangements at the time were covered unreliably by a 1933 Plymouth roadster I had bought during my freshman year. While not mechanically healthy, it was very classy. Black, with a rumble seat, twin spot lights, trumpet horns on the hood, and two spare tires sidemounted on the running boards, it would, of course, be a collectors prize today. I spent $95 for it and my father thought I'd been robbed.

* * *

June came and most of us knew that this would be our last khaki free summer. We drank too much, smoked too much, and spent too much time feeling sorry for ourselves. We really tried to enjoy an idyllic existence that summer, but we were well aware of its fragility.

Perhaps the most indelible memory I have of that endgame was sitting with Trudy on her grand porch very late at night, smoking a last cigarette, and listening to Sinatra sing "But Look at Me Now," and Jimmy Dorsey's arrangement of "Green Eyes." The romanticism of that music was a perfect reflection of a country at war.

CHAPTER 3

One day the mailman delivered a government letter to our house that familiarly began with the word, "Greetings"—a salutation that was being echoed in so many millions of American homes that even radio comedians no longer mentioned it. The letter directed me to report to my Chicago draft board on a date a few weeks hence. The die was finally cast.

Most of my friends were receiving similar little notes from Uncle Sam. Some were in ROTC programs and would follow up the specialty they had been trained for. Some would enlist in the Navy or the Marines and some would just wait to be drafted. Eventually, everybody I knew went into service. WW II was unlike the Korean War, or Vietnam, or the Gulf War. We all may have grumbled about the details, but everyone eventually understood the enormity of what was happening. It was a matter of survival. It was a them-or-us conflict. As Studs Terkel was to write fifty years later, it was the "Good War."

I had seen posters that urged me to "Be An Army Flyer" or shouted "Youth of America—Your Future Is in the Air." This seemed at the time to make sense, so I headed downtown to enlist. (It would be many months later, on a particularly nasty mission over Germany, that I would understand the dimensions of my naiveté.)

The Aviation Cadet Examining Board was in the old Post Office building on Clark Street. A vast crowd of young men was there, all apparently hoping to "Be An Army Flyer." After signing the appropriate forms, we were given a special intelligence test—similar, but more difficult than the widely used Army General Classification Test. Some hours later the scores were posted and I must modestly report that my name led all the rest.

I could already feel the powerful throb of a Pratt & Whitney engine in my very own fighter plane as I skillfully maneuvered to shoot down my Nazi enemy. Those who had passed—a moderate number—were told to report the next day to the flight surgeon's office for physical exams. I had told no one about my intentions. I wanted to be sure I could get into the Air Corps before I went blabbing about it.

The doctors poked and prodded and I was doing splendidly with every probe until we reached the scale. It showed, to my utter dismay and embarrassment, that I was eight pounds over the maximum weight allowed for my height. I was informed by a medical captain that I could either give up the idea of the Air Corps, or lose those eight pounds in the next ten days.

As the captain spoke those woeful words, a lieutenant, accompanied by a nondescript civilian, walked into the room. Because it was such a pivotal moment, I still remember much of the conversation.

"This is Mr. so-and-so of the *Chicago Daily News*." said the lieutenant, who I later learned was a public relations officer (PRO). "The paper wants a story on the relentless determination of some kid to overcome all obstacles that might keep him from serving his country." In other words, a young man who can shoulder his way into a very picky Air Corps.

They probably had more serious obstacles in mind than overweight, but the captain was busy—there were, after all, hundreds of resolute recruits streaming through his office every day. He thought for a minute and looked at me.

"Okay," he said, "Let's show how this young man can take off a few pounds just because he's so eager to do his patriotic duty."

With that, the PRO, the newsman, and I, were dismissed.

We re-grouped in the corridor. The wheels were almost visibly turning in the PRO's head. He and the news guy decided to take me to a club somewhere and get some photos of me exercising.

We jumped in a cab. A few minutes later we were in front of the Lake Shore Athletic Club. The lieutenant was apparently a member—I'm sure the newsman wasn't—and by now, a photographer had appeared. We went directly to the gym. I was issued a pair of shorts and was soon being photographed holding the oars of a rowing machine, lifting a medicine ball, pulling on weighted cables, and riding a stationary bike. I must point out that I did not actually exercise, and I certainly didn't work up a sweat. It was simply a series of carefully posed photo opportunities.

Then it was back to the recruiting office for some pictures of me on the scales. Since we hadn't photographed a "before" shot, we simply did the "before" and "after" photos at the same time, but from different angles. I in my underwear, along with a beaming medical captain, was featured in both. One last picture was taken as soon as I had dressed. It showed me signing the recruitment papers held by the still beaming captain. It was, happily enough, the only photo that was authentic. Everybody was pleased—the *Chicago Daily News*, the captain, the PRO, the Air Corps, and of course, me. I was now, for better or for worse, in the Army Air Corps. I was, of course, still eight pounds overweight.

A few days later, a document arrived reassuring me that I could go back to school and probably even graduate—a cloudy crystal ball indeed—and that I should certainly expect that the army would keep in touch. In retrospect, this does seem a rather leisurely approach for a nation fighting for its life, but at the time it must have appeared to be perfectly reasonable.

And some time later, the Saturday edition of the *News* appeared, containing a full page rotogravure spread of me rowing and lifting and bicycling and looking like I was sweating, and of course being weighed. The captions were extravagant, with applause for the young man who showed such grit in his steadfastness to serve his country. Even my parents, who were less than pleased about my Air Corps decision, could not help but be impressed with the press I had received.

It was the end of the summer and one last party, a sort of symbolic farewell, was planned. On a warm evening, several dozen of us gathered for a bittersweet picnic. Most of our crowd, at least the men, would not see each other again for years—and in several instances, ever.

* * *

Abruptly, a few weeks into the new school term, the Letter arrived. In fact, several thousand letters arrived the same day on the Purdue campus. The U.S. Army Air Corps had decided that even though its training pipeline was full, it would call up the tens of thousands of waiting recruits and stack them—warehouse them was perhaps a better way to put it—until there were available places for them to be usefully trained. At this point—February of 1943—because an invasion of Europe was still too far in the future, Churchill and Roosevelt had promised Stalin that they would greatly expand the day and night bombing of German industry. It was hoped that this pressure would help reduce German air attacks on the Soviet front. Hence, the earlier-than-planned call up of all Air Corps enlistees.

(Also at this point, the WW II news was calamitous. The Japanese had overcome most of Southeast Asia. In Africa, German troops under Rommel, were pushing the British army eastward toward Egypt. A massive German army was nearing Stalingrad.)

My letter contained orders to report to Fort Benjamin Harrison, Indianapolis in ten days. There was an immediate and palpable flurry of campus activity that morning. On the steps of most of the lecture halls, small knots of excited students were talking, fantasizing, doom-saying, and otherwise contemplating their military futures.

Along with the others, I quickly withdrew from school and loaded up my old jalopy with five semesters of books, clothes, and odds and ends, and headed for Chicago. This trip resulted in some new automotive malfunctions, but after a few extra hours of scotch-taping, I finally made it. The next morning, I drove my trusty, but tired, Plymouth to the nearest used car dealer and sold it, with a feeling of liberation, for a princely $15.

I wandered aimlessly around Chicago. I saw some movies, read some books, and foresightedly, stuffed myself with good food. At last, on the day before the appointed day, I took a train to Indianapolis. My parents saw me off at the old Illinois Central station on 12th Street and Michigan. I was naturally excited, but to them, it was an event that must have matched Agamemnon's departure to the Trojan Wars.

I spent that night at the Indy Claypool hotel—in a not-very-clean "sample room" that some traveling salesman had wisely abandoned. The next morning, bright and early, I took a bus to Fort Ben Harrison and joined many hundreds of other anxious new soldiers. Our paperwork was quickly processed and we were loaded onto a waiting train that was headed we knew not where. I was still not old enough to vote, but I was off to war.

CHAPTER 4

The lack of awareness as to where I was going, was to become routine throughout my military career. For reasons that escape me even today, the destination of a trainload of brand new recruits bound for basic training was a military secret. Everyone in the Army knew it, everyone with the railroad knew it, everyone along the way knew it, and as I found out a year or so later, even the Germans knew it. The only positive aspect to this cryptic operation was that we—that is the participants—were endlessly occupied in trying to guess just where the hell we were going. It became a wonderful game. No rumor was too wild; no inside information was disputed.

We traveled in antique day coaches, dirty at the outset of our journey and far dirtier by the end. We were distributed three to a pair of double seats facing each other. At night, we would take turns partially stretching out to sleep, one guy leaving the seats to pace the aisles or stand in the vestibule for an hour. Some people slept on the really gross floors. This would become our standard method of train travel for the next many months.

I discovered, early on, that volunteering for kitchen police

(KP) duty had certain advantages. Volunteering in the Army was almost always considered a bad idea and I learned to be very selective. KP on that train, meant working in a separate boxcar with only a few other guys, lots of time to sit and watch the scenery through open doors, and a chance to walk through the entire train without being questioned by the ubiquitous MPs. Somehow, a four hour shift made the trip go faster.

All of us were still in our civilian duds—many of us had reported for duty in suits and ties. There were no showers, of course, and we had only a few minutes a day at a washstand. We became progressively grimier and our clothes more slovenly. No one had thought to bring much reading matter so we had to trade books and magazines (many pornographic) back and forth. There was, however, no shortage of card games. It was here that I began to learn the intricacies of five-card stud and spit-in-the-ocean. Some of the games, which typically used a suitcase for a table, went on for days. Plainly, the money in use, a finite amount, was constantly being recycled.

As with all good things, as well as the not so good, this trip came to an end. Those of us whose turn it was to sleep, awoke one morning as the train lurched to a stop. We had been aware for several days that we were moving south—the red clay of rural Georgia and later, the palm trees of Florida, made our whereabouts roughly obvious. But now we saw a large station and many uniformed soldiers and we realized that wherever we were, we were there—unwashed and unhinged. It turned out to be Army Air Force Basic Training at Miami Beach, some 1200 miles from Indianapolis, and it had only taken us six days and five nights to get here.

* * *

We disembarked, our eyes blinking in the unaccustomed glare of a Miami sun. Our names were read and groups of us were loaded into Army trucks. I found myself with guys whose names all began with the letter A. (The faces might change along with my various assignments, but until my final graduation, I would always be bunking with the A's.) The trucks soon deposited sixty of us in a small ocean front hotel at the far south, and quite unfashionable, end of the Beach. Under different circumstances, it would have been a lovely vacation spot, but the weather happened to be going through an extended cold spell, and anyway, this was not supposed to be a vacation.

Our daily routine was not imaginative. We had endless hours of close-order drill. This may have been useful for new arrivals who had never enjoyed the opportunity before, but for those of us with two years of college ROTC, it was excessive. It was the Army's first shot at turning our ragged group of civilians into some semblance of tolerable soldiers. Ragged is not a bad usage here, because over the next ten days, our group—picturesquely called a squadron—was drilled, still in our original civvies. We were, to say the least, gamy.

We endured physical training (PT). We had classes in military courtesy, Army nomenclature, and first aid. We walked around policing the grounds, the streets, and the beach. We were taught that if something was growing, to leave it alone; if it was not growing, to pick it up; and if it was moving, to salute it. We attended graphic films in glowing Technicolor about what could happen to our "privates" if we fooled around with girls—any girls. These so-called VD movies were actually enjoyed by some guys, but occasionally caused others to throw up.

But mostly, we drilled and waited around. This latter activity was especially important to know about since it would become the most familiar part of our future training.

The day came at last, and we were marched to the quartermaster building and outfitted with GI clothes. It took the better part of the day and achieving even an approximate fit was chancy. We were issued several sets of summer suntans and winter olive-drab shirts and trousers, khaki undershirts, shorts, socks and handkerchiefs. GI shoes, the hiking kind, were especially difficult and many of us went through several pairs, each accompanied by a set of blisters, before we hit the right size. We also drew a heavy winter overcoat, prophetic of weather to come, a neat looking field jacket, and some caps. Lastly, came a one-piece set of greenish overalls called fatigues. None of these garments carried any insignia.

Back at our hotel, we dressed, looked in our mirrors, looked at each other, and finally realized we were in the Army. We were in uniform, we were privates and we were not to forget it. Our monthly pay was now a handsome $50. Some guys sent home what remained of their civvies. I bundled up my blue serge suit and cast it into a waste container.

* * *

There were 100,000 of us in Miami Beach. It was a basic training post as well as a holding depot. The Army had simply taken over most of the hotels in this famous and immense center of vacation resorts. It is hard to realize when you stroll around the Beach today that there were tens of thousands of uniformed men walking those same streets in the winter of 1943. The celebrated Miami Beach was, in effect, the Army Air Corps, although we never saw an airplane, nor heard a lecture about anything concerning the air. Non-commissioned officers, mostly corporals and a few buck sergeants, made up the entire staff.

Another exciting feature of Miami Beach, of course, was the presence of German submarines off the Florida coast. It surely brought the war closer to all of us when the black smoke visible on the horizon was a torpedoed U.S. tanker.

After a few weeks, we became eligible for passes on those evenings when there were no classes and no "GI Parties" scheduled. A GI Party, for the uninitiated, was an obligatory scrubbing, on hands and knees, of every surface of a barracks—or in this case a hotel.

Few of the guys made use of the passes since there was really no place to go. There were no bars nearby and no transportation to get anywhere. At our end of the Beach, there was a popular dog track and some of us visited that a few times. It turned out to be an expensive and unexciting experience. Watching dogs chase a fake, electrically powered rabbit is not exactly the sport of kings.

As it happened, I had a distinct advantage over the khaki crowd. My paternal grandmother and my aunt had an apartment not far from our hotel. They had lived there for years, although never before surrounded by 100,000 soldiers, and I, of course, was invited for as many dinners as I could arrange. Unhappily, these were few, but it was still nice to go somewhere civilian-like for a few hours to relax and have some non-army chow.

The Air Corps had adopted the Army model of basic training, and the Army, of course, was busily drafting millions of kids. The vast majority of them had gone no farther than high school, and many not that far. Viewed in perspective, Miami Beach was what today would be called a boot camp—a rather mild version, but enormous in size. What we did and learned in six weeks, could have been accomplished in two, but it's important to remember that this was just a year after Pearl Harbor—and America was building what would soon become an armed force of over sixteen million men. In training terms, sheer weight seemed more meaningful than simple efficiency.

It was also about this time that the army changed the designation of its air arm from the Army Air Corps to the Army Air Forces. Years later, in 1947, Congress would establish the Air Force as an entirely separate branch of the armed services, but for the balance of my military career, I was a member of the U.S. Army Air Forces.

*   *   *

In late March, and as usual with little notice, our small hotel cadre was ordered to scrub our rooms, bathrooms, and all of the hotel lobby. Joining some other groups, we were loaded onto a train and two days later, after endless and sometimes acerbic arguments and continuous wagers, we found ourselves, to our total astonishment, in Pittsburgh, Pennsylvania.

Chapter 5

We were now assigned to a College Training Detachment (CTD) and would call the University of Pittsburgh our new home. This was another holding pool for the men who had been called up for active duty but could not yet be fitted into the pipeline. Since the Air Force was no longer demanding college graduates, as it had up until Pearl Harbor, and since most U.S. colleges had a good deal of space available those days, the higher-ups decided that a few weeks of college training couldn't hurt.

The U of P was a unique school. Its home was a single high-rise building, called somewhat grandly, the Cathedral of Learning. Several floors had been set aside for us and soon we were sleeping, eating, and attending classes in an elevator environment. On nice days, we would go outside for our drills and physical training, but on dark April days, we would never see the sky. Our routine was more varied than it had been in Miami Beach, but it was still a routine. Up early, clean, sweep, breakfast, class, PT, lunch, class, drill, dinner, study, bed. Easy enough to get used to, but in Pittsburgh it involved over a dozen elevator rides with interminable waits.

After two months of repetitive drilling and irrelevant learning, we abruptly left Pittsburgh. It had not been unpleasant duty. The food was good and the surroundings were—well—collegiate. Most of us though, were impatiently ready to go to war.

* * *

We were once more back in the Army Air Forces loop. We were back in the inexorable progression of steps leading to combat. This next step was the AAF Classification Center in Nashville.

Although we were excited about moving on, we were aware from the usual grapevine that we were trading a very cushy, civilian-like post for a stereotypical, real army base. We were not wrong. Nashville was a sea of mud, punctuated by uncountable raw wood barracks, god-awful food, and thousands of restless guys.

Here, over a short period of two weeks—which would seem like two months—the incoming trainees were to be classified as pilots, navigators or bombardiers. We would be psychologically, intellectually, and physically probed, massaged, mined, and rummaged through. When we left here most of us would be Aviation Cadets. The system was purported to be a state-of-the-art, scientifically valid method of placing round pegs into round holes. As we would one day comprehend, it was not. The process was governed by supply and demand. It was totally connected to the war.

* * *

So let the games begin. This battery of tests, nationally known because of so many thrilling movies and in depth magazine stories, was both exhaustive and exhausting. First, came the so-called mental exams. Eight hours of sitting at screened-off desks—to prevent cheating—in 90 degrees of humid air. The tests covered every kind of material, mostly immaterial, that the Air Force, could conjure up.

Then came the psychological probing. Playing with pieces of wood, for example, or being timed at putting a puzzle together. This led to interviews with an Army psychiatrist who, in a half-hour or so, was expected to know more about me than I did. Preposterous!

Last came the physicals that included everything that any doc could have ever conceived. It made my enlistment exams seem like a cursory checkup. Someone counted thirty-four doctors present. A complete eye exam took place in four rooms and absorbed the attentions of seven docs. A dentist looked into my mouth; an ear, nose, and throat specialist looked into his dominions; The X-ray guys, the lung experts, the heart thumpers, the anus and genitalia examiners—all plied their trades.

When it was time to be weighed, my heart was in my mouth, but because of the rigors of floor scrubbing and the turn-offs of crappy food, I sailed through with the lowest number of my life, an emaciated 192 pounds—six under the max. I heaved a mighty sigh of relief and staggered to the "summing-up" doctor and then we all marched to our barracks. It would be another week before we would know our military future.

* * *

The tests were over, but not the heavy lifting. Each of us was regularly assigned to some disagreeable task. I was on latrine cleaning detail. I was on grass cutting and area policing. I pulled guard duty. But most awesome of all was the Kitchen Police. The Classification Center was immense and there was but one mess hall for trainees.

My first KP detail began at 4:00a.m. and lasted fourteen hours through three full meals. Rather than washing dishes or pots and pans (called pearl diving) or scrubbing messy mess hall floors, I lucked out as a cook's helper and spent that long day helping to prepare a veritable mountain of food. For example, I was involved in the grinding of a thousand pounds of beef to be used in meat sauce. I helped crack open some 3600 eggs for breakfast. I assisted in the baking of seventy-four huge hams. These were Brobdingnagian portions, but unhappily, when that food finally reached our plates, it was far less than appetizing.

It was time to ship out of this glorious vacation spot. Oh yes. I'd been classified as a pilot. After the many batteries of sophisticated tests to determine whether my skills would be best used as a pilot, navigator, bombardier, or simply an aerial gunner, an interesting phenomenon had occurred. It seemed that the Air Force needed huge numbers of pilots, so all of us, and many of the groups which followed us, were hastily classified as pilots, our talents notwithstanding.

The only surprising aspect to this bureaucratic decision was that we were at all surprised. Anyone familiar with Air Force requirements must have known that on heavy bombers, for each bombardier and navigator, there were two pilots, and then, of course, there were the thousands of light bombers, fighter planes, transports, and so on. Tens of thousands of pilots were being trained all over the U.S. If so many pilots were needed, why did the generals think it was so important to maintain this cumbersome and expensive classification center in Nashville? We'll never know.

But what I did know as summer approached was that I was going to be, one way or another, an army flyer. I was going to war.

We left Nashville—the town I never saw—with no regrets. We were now Aviation Cadets on our way to becoming flying officers and even our pay reflected our lofty status, rocketing to $75 a month. Our shiny new insignia was issued and I cannot believe I became so excited about those modest trinkets being affixed to my collar and sleeve.

CHAPTER 6

Maxwell Field, the Army Air Forces' preflight school, was an old established Army post in Montgomery, Alabama, it would be an important stop on my military itinerary, but my fellow cadets and I were caught off guard.

As we disembarked from our Nashville train, we were immediately initiated into the recondite ceremonies of the cadet structure of that time.

As I climbed down the steps, travel-soiled and overtired, a crisply dressed cadet with some stripes on his sleeve confronted me.

"Mister," he shouted, "Get those shoulders back. Suck in that gut. Tuck in your chin. Look me in the eye. Brace!" I was to hear the word "brace" a hundred times a day, but this first time was the most startling. We underclassmen were the West Point Plebes and the VMI Rats of the Air Force and we were quickly made to understand there would be no swift relief from this molestation. For four weeks, we must withstand a rigid regime of hazing and its accompanying punishments, and there would be precious few rewards. The following month, however, as upperclassmen, we could pass on the fine points of the program to a new crop of underclassmen.

This was the upper class/lower class cadet system, copied from West Point and shortened from two years to two months. Its mission was to turn out officers and gentlemen. It was totally inappropriate for a wartime Air Force charged with training a hundred thousand new flyers each year.

So pay attention to what I am saying. Lower classmen were lower than the red Alabama soil. We popped to attention and braced whenever an upper classman walked into our room, which was, as ill luck would have it, quite often. We looked straight ahead and never deviated our gaze—or let our "eyeballs click"—while walking or marching or eating or talking to an upperclassman. Because of this mandatory stare, we were called "Zombies," and surely we must have resembled the living dead.

There were only three answers allowed when spoken to: "Yes sir," "No sir," and "No excuse sir."

If we were foolish enough to want to say something or perhaps ask a question, we had to sound off—"Sir, Aviation Cadet Alter, J.M., requests permission to make a statement (or ask a question)" There were no exceptions to this rule and it did tend to restrain conversation. In addition, there was an inexhaustible supply of definitions, soliloquies, and nonsense lines to sound off with on command. For example, if we were asked how we felt, we first requested permission to speak and then would say, "Miserable, but proud, Sir."

We learned to stand straight as a broom handle, wipe all traces of a smile off our faces, and walk the "rat line" which was the long way to any point. The rat line included making military corners at every turn and "driving," that is walking as fast as possible without actually running. We had to be at every scheduled formation at least five minutes early, with shoes shined like mirrors, nails cleaned, hair combed, and all clothing perfectly adjusted. There we stood, while the upperclassmen walked around us making contemptuous comments and yelling in our ears. There were some eight or ten of these formations a day with only a few minutes to prepare for each.

At Maxwell, everything was on the double. "Brace, Mister. Drive, Mister." And, I cannot resist adding, that this was summertime in the Deep South and the temperature rarely left the nineties. Hence, another command frequently heard, as our shirts darkened with perspiration, was, "Mister, stop sweating." And while I did my best to do what I was told, the inner me was also steamimg. Who were these assholes, just one month my seniors, to manipulate me this way?

Meals were a ritual by themselves. Whenever we wanted something on the table, we sounded off with, "Sirs, does anyone care for mashed potatoes—may I help myself?" We ate "square meals." That is, we sat straight and lifted our fork vertically to the height of our mouths and then brought it in horizontally. If we spilled, we cried, "Sirs, I'm a gross dribbler—dribble, dribble, dribble." If we made a noise by dropping something, we said, "Sirs, I'm a gross racketeer—racket, racket, racket."

Whether any of this foolishness helped end the war, I leave to the military historians.

* * *

The above described regimen which some might call discipline and others simply nonsense, was fortunately not the central feature of our time at Maxwell Field. Although we may have devoted a good deal of our efforts to avoiding upperclassmen, the real thrust of our mission here was to prepare ourselves for pilot training and officerhood. There was more than enough of this to keep us busy.

There were classes in code, aircraft identification, first aid, military sanitation, chemical warfare, math, physics and more. These subjects were not, at least for me, much of a stretch. I had already learned in ROTC at Purdue that during each class, a military instructor would always emphasize the answers to the questions he intended to ask on the test for that day. My grades were exemplary

The one exception was code. We would sit in a large room with earphones and a pad and pencil. As the dots and dashes filtered through our ears, we would write down each word. The official requirement to pass this new vernacular was eight words a minute and it was not an effortless exercise. I had never been good at foreign languages, nor did I have an ear for music, and I found that translating code demanded similar witchcraft.

The other serious challenge to my native abilities was physical. Similar to what we had suffered at previous posts, we once again underwent daily calisthenics, a diabolic obstacle course, and long daily runs. Maxwell also offered something extra. It was called the "Burma Road" and it must have been conceived by an athletic Martian.

We would run a mile to a thickly wooded area. We would then run two miles on the "Road." It was a narrow trail that wound its way over alpine-like hills, down precipitous ravines, and back and forth through a wide stream bed. Then, facing total exhaustion, we would run a mile back to the barracks. And all of this, as I will continue to mention, in a moist blanket of summer-in-Alabama heat. We survived this with the help of tons of water and salt pills. When we finally reached home—if you will pardon the euphemism—we had a bare five minutes to showerlessly change into our uniforms, and face the torment of the upperclassmen as we formed our ranks for lunch. "Brace and stop sweating, Mister," they would say.

* * *

While we were underclassmen, our Sunday mornings were just as structured as the rest of the week. Attendance at the church services of our choice was compulsory. After breakfast, we reported to one of three groups. We were either Catholic, Protestant, or Jewish. I have no idea where Moslems, Hindus, or Buddhists went. My first week, I joined the small Jewish group. (after all, my dog tag did have an "H" on it.) Under the usual summer sun, we marched for what seemed miles to the far end of the post. We entered a small temporary building which had been designated as an all purpose synagogue.

It was my first Orthodox service and I sat through nearly two hours, almost entirely in Hebrew, sweltering in an unairconditioned, uninsulated, overcrowded room. Then there was the long march back. This religious experience had, as far as I was concerned, squandered three hours of time that I could ill afford.

Later, in the barracks, we pilgrims of the three religions compared notes. The Protestants also had had a long walk and had expended several hot hours that morning, but the Catholics, because their assigned church happened to be across the road from our barracks, had ambled home in less than an hour. The following Sunday, I fell out with the Catholics. I assured myself I was neither being proselytized nor converted, but had simply become a seeker of convenience.

* * *

June ended and we were now—we could hardly believe it—upperclassmen. There was a traditional Really Big Inspection which required two days of scouring and primping. It was rigorous. I was gigged for forgetting to button my trousers, which were hanging under my shirt, which was hanging under my raincoat, which was hanging in my closet.

There was a Really Big Parade to honor the graduating class. That class, our erstwhile tormentors, after a recognition ceremony, shook hands with us, apologized for being so offensive, and left the squadron in our care. The new class of zombies arrived and they were very gross. As upperclassmen, it was now our duty to straighten them out.

A tough job, but someone had to do it. So now we could amuse ourselves by bracing the new guys and making sure that their eyeballs didn't click and that they were miserable but proud.

*   *   *

Three days before our graduation from preflight school, I felt unwell. I reported to Sick Call and was diagnosed as having bronchitis. Since the Army considered me infectious, I was hustled to the base hospital. One of my roommates brought me some necessaries and bade me goodbye. My class was going to flight school without me.

My week in the hospital was, except for my disappointment about not moving on, a total joy. I slept a lot, read four or five books, talked to some interesting guys, flirted with two pretty nurses, and in general was as happy as a not-very-sick clam. When I was discharged, I walked back to my old barracks and naturally, there were no familiar faces.

Eventually, I was directed to a special barracks, known familiarly, and not too inaccurately, as the Fuck-Up House. It was the temporary resting place for pariahs, wash outs, misfits, and renegades. It was also where unfortunates, such as me, who had inadvertently missed their class, were assigned. We would be shipping out with the next class in about three weeks.

Three weeks! Wow! How about some leave? I ultimately found an officer who gave me a stack of papers to fill out and said I could get a ten day furlough if everything "worked." So I made the rounds. I took a makeup test here, a final exam there, and a dreaded code assessment somewhere. I passed everything. I got waivers and releases and passes and documents in fine print. And at last I got a piece of paper that said ten days writ large. I took a bus into town and caught the evening train to Chicago—this time Pullman since I was paying. As I sat luxuriously in the diner, I drank a special toast to those innocent little germs that had put me where I was.

*　　*　　*

It was a wonderful leave. Because of the rigors of the Burma Road and other Maxwell Field excesses, I was as slim as I would ever be. I was tanned and quite spiffy in my cadet regalia, which did a good deal for my Army-suppressed ego. I did have to be careful at dinner parties not to revert to earlier Army habits by asking someone to pass the fucking butter.

I spent a good deal of time wandering around in downtown Chicago. It had been just six months since I had left town, but the changes were startling. Now it really seemed that America was at war. Except for the very young and the very old, nearly every male—and a good number of females—was in some kind of uniform. Sailors from the Great Lakes Naval Base, soldiers from Fort Sheridan, officers from various training centers, and thousands of guys on leave or passing through. Even my mother was in a Red Cross uniform.

Meanwhile, German forces in North Africa surrender. The battle of Kursk, the greatest tank engagement in history, is won by the Soviets. Sicily is invaded by the Allies.

CHAPTER 7

In due course, I headed back to Maxwell, spent a few days practicing code and running the Burma Road, and soon was on my way to a Primary Flying School—Carlstrom Field in Arcadia, Florida.

All Army Air Forces primary training was contracted out to civilian flying schools. There was an interesting arithmetical logic to this. The Army needed many pilots. It had already recruited thousands of eager young men and had tested, probed and prodded them at classification centers such as Nashville as best an army could. The top brass were aware, however, that no matter what their scientific tests showed, many of these embryonic pilots were simply not going to make it. Flying required certain elusive skills that were not so easily measured.

Rather than build hundreds of new airfields from scratch, just to discover who could or couldn't fly, the Air Forces farmed out the job to the hundreds of already existing civilian fields. This also meant that instead of becoming primary instructors, thousands of already trained Army pilots could do what they were supposed to do—go fight a war.

Once the Army knew which of their beginners could

actually fly an airplane, it sent them on to more advanced training. These were real Army Air Forces installations, but there were fewer of them than the primary fields and it was at these posts that our future military pilots were actually produced.

Physically, Carlstrom Field was plain and unvarnished. The Riddle Aeronautical Institute which operated it, had quickly built non-army type cottages, billeting three cadets to a room, each with its own bath. It was undreamt of luxury. The food was great, the water sulphurous, and the mosquitoes energetic. As with most of the posts we occupied in this long continuum of becoming airmen, we were busy as hell. We had few free moments and took much tougher classes.

* * *

The academic content here was germane. We learned the theory of flight—airfoils, lift ratios, and other complex aerodynamics. We had hours of aircraft engine design and maintenance—compression, horsepower measurement, fire protection, and the like.

Half of every day—about five hours—was spent on the flight line. We either flew, watched other guys fly, or did homework. Each civilian instructor had five students. We would fly once, and were expected to meet our airplane whenever it landed to help get it ready for the next flight. After a flight, a stack of forms had to be filled out with such details as takeoff and landing times, an analysis of our mistakes, our suggested corrections, and so on.

My first day in the air was eventful. It also happened to be the first flight of my life. The instructor carefully explained all the instruments and controls. He helped me adjust my parachute and showed me how to fasten the seat belt. Even this was new to me since automobiles at that time did not have seat belts. It was all pretty fundamental stuff—

almost like the Wright brothers. (Now that I think of it, this 1943 afternoon was much closer to Orville and Wilbur's first flight than to my most recent jet flight to Newark.)

We were flying Stearman PT-17s, an open cockpit biplane only seen today in antique air shows. It was a powerful (220 HP) machine and rather large, considering it carried just two men.

The open cockpit appealed to the old convertible-lover in me. That is it did until my instructor demonstrated a snap roll, leaving me hanging upside down, held in only by my seat belt. I looked up, which was really down, and saw earth and lots of empty space. I silently hoped that the seat belt manufacturer had not been the lowest bidder.

Later, the instructor abruptly cut off the engine and indicated I should look for a place to land. "Just pretend that the engine quit and you gotta put her down," he shouted. I gazed at the rapidly approaching terra all-too-firma and vaguely pointed at some farmland in the distance. The instructor nodded his head and re-started our precious engine.

I was next shown a steep climb ending in a stall. It was like riding on a golf ball which has reached its maximum height and is poised to descend. Then, the instructor kicked the rudder and we began to spin and the ground below began doing the twist. I was by now feeling a little green, a condition that my guru noticed in his rearview mirror. He asked me, through the one-way speaking tube, how I felt and I shrugged heroically.

"A major urp will do you good." he yelled. "Is your seat belt fastened?" I just knew that some ghastly sort of exercise was coming. There was a sudden lurch and we began a series of rolls, loops, Immelmanns, and other unspeakable things that man was not put on this earth to ever face.

We leveled off and I grabbed the stick, indicating I wanted the controls. I went into a steep bank as I had been taught to do only a few minutes earlier and let go the remnants of my not inconsiderably sized lunch. My instructor's face in the mirror composed itself into a sweet smile. "Good timing. Good aim." We landed and taxied over to the water hoses where other cadets were furiously scrubbing the mementos of their first flight from the sides of their airplanes. I joined them.

* * *

Flying and ground school continued for several weeks, accompanied by periodic, and very intimidating, official flight checks. We mastered stalls, spins, dives, banks, and, of course, takeoffs and landings. Because so much was compressed into so little time, it is now a forgettable haze. Even my solo, which was certainly a signal event when it happened, has become murky. I know that I took off, circled the field, and made a shaky landing. I was then welcomed into the fraternity of airmen, and that allowed me to wear my goggles on top of my helmet instead of on the back of my neck, but I don't remember much else.

A few days later, however, came a very fateful check ride. These checks were made by Air Force officers, rather than civilian instructors, and were much dreaded. Sure enough, I blew it. The lieutenant told me to execute a two and a half turn spin. I started down, watched the earth and all the pretty farmland begin to rotate and somehow didn't choose to stop. Two turns, three turns, four turns, maybe it was autohypnosis. I'll never know. The lieutenant, naturally, was becoming restive—no, I guess he was becoming panicky. He was yelling at me and trying to get control of the stick and rudder bar, which is hard to do in a spin. Finally, well below a 1000 feet, I reluctantly gave him jurisdiction. We quickly landed and within hours, I was an ex-pilot.

After an inquiry and a meeting with my tactical officer, it was decided that because my previous achievement scores were high and because I was such a nice guy, I would be assigned to the select company of bombardiers, the true heroes of the wild blue yonder. I would eventually receive my wings and become a member of the commissioned gentry. Since I would still be an "army flyer," I suppose I was not too displeased about my fate.

CHAPTER 8

From Carlstrom Field, my train chugged on to Moody Field in Georgia where I would await my orders for gunnery school—a necessary step to becoming a bombardier. It was a pleasing respite where I managed to find a cushy job as a cadet adjutant, latch onto a girl friend, enjoy some wonderful chow, and revel in the total lack of regimen. Unfortunately, it didn't last long.

* * *

I embarked for Tyndall Field, a major training facility in the Florida panhandle near Panama City. Since every heavy bomber carried eight gunners, gunnery schools were programmed to turn out huge numbers of them as quickly as possible. There was little time for the luxurious cadet amenities that I had become so accustomed to.

The Army Air Force gunnery schools had only one mission—to teach thousands of kids how to shoot down enemy aircraft. To accomplish this admirable goal, the focus was primarily on teaching just two skills. First, the technique of leading the target that was to be shot down, and second, to learn how to disassemble and reassemble a caliber.50 machine gun under all conditions—which meant 25,000 feet and 40 degrees below zero.

* * *

For comfort, Tyndall Field was a downer. I was squeezed into a teensy room with a dozen other guys. The field itself was depressingly crowded with rough, unadorned barracks and few amenities.

In spite of the lack of any charm, gunnery school, to my surprise, turned out to be great fun. Why not? Here were all of these young guys spending their time firing a wide variety of guns and thousands and thousands of rounds of ammunition. What could be more macho, especially during a war. For the entire six weeks at Tyndall, not a day went by without a lot of shooting. It was a very noisy Disneyland—long before Disneyland had been invented.

We started with skeet. Tyndall had dozens of skeet ranges and we were divided into small groups and would shoot four rounds during a morning. Each round consisted of twenty-five shots with a twelve-gauge shotgun—a gun with a big kick. Thus, a hundred shots and some very black and blue shoulders.

From ordinary skeet, we moved on to power turrets. This was an apparatus where a twelve-gauge shotgun was mounted on an electrically powered top turret, identical to the turrets on B-24s and B-17s. The clay pigeons were released from a thirty foot tower and the shooter tried to lead them by pressing the correct buttons to swing his turret and then squeezing the trigger at exactly the right time. It was a lot harder than swinging a shotgun manually.

Next came the most sporting exercise of all. A quarter-mile circular track had been cleared in a heavily forested area. Thirty trap houses were concealed among the trees and bushes. The shooter stood on a flatbed truck with a steel railing to lean against. As the truck drove around the track, increasing its speed on each run, the clay pigeons would be released from the traps. At one stretch I remember, eight birds came at me in twenty seconds. Just to aim, lead, fire, and reload thirty times in a few minutes, was no mean feat—even if every pigeon was missed.

Besides sharpening our shooting eyes, this workout was also supposed to simulate the speed with which attacking fighters could swarm around a heavy bomber. But more than anything else, this Wild West teaching tool was the best game in town.

* * *

Some evenings, after it was too dark to shoot outside, we worked on the Waller Trainers. This early combination of a video game (before there was video) and an Imax performance (before there was Imax) consisted of a half-dozen movie projectors synchronizing a film 360 degrees on the walls and ceiling of a very large room. The gunner sat in a real turret mounted with guns that shot beams of light, and a fantastic adventure would begin. I was the tailgunner on a Flying Fortress bombing Germany. The six projectors create a three dimensional sensation. There were full sound effects of the engines roar. Suddenly, through my earphones I'd hear, "Fighters at five o'clock," and all hell broke loose. I would see an ME-109 crossing my tail and I'd open fire as it entered my sights. My guns vibrated and the noise was deafening. This went on for many minutes with fighters attacking from all angles and at all speeds. At last, the lights went on and I was back at Tyndall Field and my shirt was soaked.

This magical toy must have cost several million 1940 bucks to develop and it is hard to realize that it was all done without electronics.

* * *

About this time I had another adventure. My Commanding Officer, a second lieutenant, called me into his private quarters. He made me promise that our conversation would go no further than the room we were in. He told me that the Army had reason to believe that there were "subversive elements" scattered throughout certain military units. He asked me if I would be willing to do my patriotic duty and be an undercover operative. What could I say? He went on to explain that all I had to do was to keep my ears open for any seditious talk, either Fascist or Communist, and my eyes open for any subversive literature. I was to report such monstrous crimes promptly. In short, I was ordered to be a spy. As I look back, I'm not sure I really knew what the hell he was talking about.

The method of reporting was straight out of every espionage book ever written. I would write a weekly letter to a "friend" in Panama City, using a dumb code I no longer remember. For five weeks I sent these letters, each one reporting that I had nothing to report. I went along with this bizarre diversion because I was young, eager to please, and because my CO "asked" me to. Oh well, Nathan Hale did it too.

* * *

While all the exciting shooting was going on, we still had a lot of class work. There was code practice and aircraft recognition, but the largest slice of time was devoted to the caliber .50 machine gun. This was the Army's weapon of choice for all bomber crews. It was big, heavy, and very deadly. B-24s and B-17s each carried ten of them and they were designed to protect a bomber from attacks coming from every possible direction. As aspiring gunners, we were charged not only with learning everything there was to know about the gun, but keeping it firing no matter what malfunction might occur. This was important because even one inoperative gun could render an airplane, and by extension, an entire squadron, vulnerable.

We studied every one of the nearly fifty components that were part of the gun. We deconstructed it. We put it back together. God forbid there should be any leftover parts. If some defective components had been substituted in the pile in front of us, we must identify them. Finally came the day— the Waterloo of gunnery school—when we disassembled and then reassembled the weapon while blindfolded.

Our intimate friendship with the machine gun eventually joined our familiarity with motorized turrets. We went to a special range, sat in the turrets, and blasted moving targets with the dual guns. A dozen or so guys all firing simultaneously. Talk about noise—it was ear-splitting. The appetite for ammunition on these various ranges was massive. We were told that before we left Tyndall, we would each fire nearly 5000 rounds of shotgun and machine gun ammo. Multiply that by the thousands of men who flowed through that place and it added up to a lot of lead on a few acres.

* * *

About forty miles east of Tyndall Field lies Apalachicola, in those days a small town surrounded by a cluster of tropical islands—mostly unoccupied. Because the throngs of students at Tyndall had overwhelmed its capabilities for gunnery training in the air, a camp had been set up in this truly remote area. It was a rugged, no frills kind of post, but for a week, it was great. We learned how to fire our machine guns at very low altitudes—we were in fact, strafing—a proficiency that, in my case, was never to be used in actual combat. Because our group was relatively small, we were able to log a lot of flight time and there was a welcome relaxing of the chickenshit discipline that was so constricting back at Tyndall.

The flying was a good deal different than I had experienced in the small primary trainers at Carlstrom Field.

For one thing, of course, we weren't pilots, but merely passengers. The planes were huge—at least to us—Lockheed Hudson medium bombers, with two waist guns and a turret on top. (Waist guns are towards the rear of the plane and are fired out of large openings, one on either side.) Three students would fire and three would wait.

Some of our missions were ground strafing over water where wooden targets had been anchored. We called this business "Splash." At other times, we used cameras for more exact grading of our abilities. There was also an attempt at simulated combat with three bombers flying in formation and P-40 fighter planes diving at us from every angle as we fired our camera-guns. It was realistic and taught us the most important maxim of aerial gunnery—there is little time to shoot before you get shot.

* * *

After an exciting week at Apalachicola, we headed back to big Tyndall and prepared to graduate and move out. Our last few days were spent sitting for hours on the main flight line, awaiting our brief turn to fly in a real Flying Fortress. This B-17, which along with the B-24, was the largest WW II combat airplane used in Europe, was imposing. It carried ten men, eight gun positions, tons of bombs, and had enormous range. It was the principal heavy bomber flying out of England. The B-24 flew mostly in other combat theatres. Although I had only one ride in this colossus at Tyndall, it was thrilling. I sat in the top turret and fired at tow targets pulled at a safe distance by fighter planes. The feel of such a big aircraft would become quite familiar to me a few months later.

* * *

Graduation at last. Our silver Gunner's wings were more

or less tossed to us without ceremony because everyone was in a big rush. We packed up quickly and with few sentiments, shipped out of Tyndall Field.

Most of the newly minted cadet gunners were directed to southeastern and Texas schools, but a score of us, for the usual enigmatic military reasons, were bundled off to California. Our rail car was hitched to a number of different trains each headed west, and it took a long time. It included an all day stopover in New Orleans where I cruised, wide eyed, up and down Bourbon Street. For an untraveled greenhorn, the foreign flavor of New Orleans of the forties was irresistible. Our very slow train also offered us a not-so-interesting day in what was then a smallish city called Houston.

We hit Santa Fe quite late on Christmas Eve where I toyed with a depressing dinner served in a Fred Harvey restaurant. This was one of the few times during the war when I was genuinely homesick. Then on to a steam (yes, steam) driven train and finally we were in California—my maiden date with the Golden State—and everything was different. We were now at the Victorville Army Flying School, a large airbase near a small town, and one of the principal bombardier training facilities of the Western Command. We were in the Mohave Desert, and only a couple of hours from Los Angeles.

CHAPTER 9

There are several things to be said about Victorville right at the outset. First, I was to be there for nearly four months—the longest posting in my Army career thus far. This field would also be the venue for my transition from cadet to flying officer, assuming, of course, that I cleared all the hurdles. And lastly, Victorville was hands down, the most comfortable station I had yet experienced. The food was sensational, the ambience pleasant, and the work was exciting and directly relevant to our anticipated military goal—helping to win the war.

The course covered eighteen weeks, six of navigation and twelve of bombing. We started out with a number of new possessions. There were fleece-lined clothes, fancy sun glasses, two precision watches, charts, manuals, and a calculator called the E-6B computer, (this was years before real computers) which could figure everything from wind drift to airspeed variations.

Since we would soon be privy to a good deal of classified information—much of it concerning the hallowed Norden bombsight—we answered endless questions about our background, loyalty quotient, and other private matters.

Months later, my parents wrote me that an FBI man had actually visited our Chicago apartment as part of this routine investigation.

It was now New Years Day of 1944 and this was my ninth post in ten months. Although I didn't know it yet, before the year was over, I would be in the real honest-to-goodness war. I would be dropping bombs on Nazi Germany. My tenth combat mission would be flown while still in this calendar year.

* * *

On New Years Eve, several of us, overnight passes in hand, headed for the Los Angeles. We stood on the side of the road with our thumbs extended and were quickly invited to join a young officer in a big hurry. We had already heard that in order to save gas, one could coast a long way down from Cajon Pass, but this guy was able to stretch it out to thirty-two miles with his ignition off—a record of sorts. This obliged him to disregard his brakes and use up in rubber what he'd saved in gas. Our screeching turns around thousand foot chasms kept reminding me that we had left our parachutes back at the base. We reached L.A. in no time and were dropped off in Hollywood.

On this night, of course, we did clubs and bars, lots and lots of them. Around three in the morning, we began to wonder where we might find a place to sleep for a few hours. By a fortunate coincidence, a guy standing at the bar heard me wondering and offered us a pad. We walked a few blocks and there was the stereotypical, albeit rundown, Hollywood mansion in all of its pink stucco glory. It belonged to a long faded silent screen star, whose name we never did catch, who was having a major kind of party—or maybe closer to an orgy. There seemed to be bodies locked together everywhere—in the cavernous living room, any number of parlors, the billiard room, and several unidentified chambers.

We met a few folks and partied another hour or so, and were finally referred to the library, where we flopped down on some couches and slept until breakfast, which was served promptly at 1 p.m. At least a dozen guests were still there, and in the cold light of day, we noticed that most of them were men. Obviously, as far as Los Angeles society was concerned, I was still on a learning curve.

* * *

Navigation ground school was difficult, but lively. I did a few things wrong, but that's the way we're supposed to learn—right? Somewhat to my surprise, I enjoyed the demands of navigation. It was hard work and required meticulous attention to detail. But it had the fascination of exactness—that is, if you did everything just right, you knew precisely where you were on the map and precisely when you would get to where you were going. I only occasionally did everything just right.

The question often came up as to why we fledgling bombardiers were being burdened with six weeks of navigational training. Bombardiers were still urgently needed in Europe and the Pacific, so why hold them up this way? There were two answers. First, there had always been a good deal of cross training for air crews. In certain situations, it might be essential for one crewman to be able to fill in for another.

Second, as more sophisticated aerial tactics developed, it had been found that only the lead and deputy lead planes in a squadron or group needed both a bombardier and a navigator. The rest of the airplanes simply followed along and salvoed their bombs when the lead ship did. Thus, those crews that were following required only one man up in the

Plexiglas nose. Obviously that guy needed navigational training because, if for any number of reasons, an airplane became separated from its squadron, someone had to be prepared to find the way home.

After a few weeks of simulated navigation as groundlings, we enthusiastically took to the air. On a typical mission, two cadets, an instructor, and the pilot would climb aboard the airplane, a twin-engine AT-11 which was used for all navigator, bombardier, and advanced pilot training. One cadet sat up in the glass nose doing pilotage and the other was aft in an area without windows, practicing dead reckoning (DR).

Pilotage is the business of keeping track of where the airplane is by comparing what you see on the ground with what is shown on the map. If, for example, I saw a power plant below me and could match it to a symbol on my map, I would know exactly where I was, whether I was on the proper course, and how far it was to my destination. These so-called landmarks might be towns, lakes, bridges, roads—almost any feature that could be seen from the air and identified on a map.

Dead reckoning, on the other hand, was a more intellectual, and almost abstract exercise. I would sit at a small desk, watching the compass and the airspeed indicator, and using a drift meter to try and judge the wind direction and velocity, (This was a telescopic instrument aimed straight down to the ground and was designed to gauge the airplane's actual drift.) Every five minutes, I would enter the headings, air speed, altitude, and drift into my log and work ahead on my actual course. I would give the pilot any course corrections that I thought were necessary. In effect, I was guiding the airplane.

On our training flights, we two cadets would trade places at the halfway point, so that I might dead reckon to Boulder Dam, for example, and then use pilotage to return home. Of these two methods of navigation, (There was also a third procedure called celestial which establishes one's position by measuring the angles of known stars or the sun using an octant, and a fourth which used a radio compass.) I found pilotage the more difficult. It took a good deal of practice to recognize landmarks from several thousand feet up.

On actual operational missions, the navigator combined these two methods. He would sit in the nose with a map and try to match what he saw on the ground with what was on his map. But he also used his instruments and maintained his log so that if clouds should suddenly obscure the ground, he could still, by dead reckoning, maintain his heading.

Our training flights took us over most of the Southern California landscape—Death Valley, Palm Springs, San Diego, and countless mountains, and deserts. We might fly a two or three part mission hoping against hope that we would hit each destination with exactitude. We thought of ourselves as fastidiously precise, but we were still pretty sloppy. For one thing, as the ground rolled relentlessly beneath us, the five minute readings and log entries seemed to come every couple of seconds, and we'd fall behind as they piled up on each other.

Sometimes everything on the ground would look like everything else. I'd be in the middle of a computation and the instructor would holler over the intercom, "Where are we?" Once, early in my training, as we were crossing a river, I told him we were over the Colorado, and the gentle lieutenant screamed, "For Christ's sake, the Colorado runs through five states, which one are we in?" But things did begin to look up as I became more accustomed to looking down.

CHAPTER 10

As our navigation training flights continued, our bombardier ground school classes began. First, came the theory of bombing—how altitude, temperature, airspeed, and wind direction affect the downward path of a bomb, and the computations and tables which determine when to release said bomb.

And then there was the bombsight itself. Built by the Norden Company at a cost of $14,000 each (1944 dollars), and developed by engineers, mathematicians, and physicists, the bombsight was, in those pre-electronic, non-transistorized, totally chipless days, a mechanical—almost Rube Goldbergish—*tour de force*.

An electric spinning gyroscope kept the bombsight level, and a built-in control, hooked up to the airplane's autopilot, allowed the bombardier to steer the plane to the left or right. Most ingenious was a system that when all the variables (speed, wind, altitude, etc.) had been fed into it, the device would compute the precise moment to release the bombs. The bombardier's job was simply to peer through the bombsight at his target, turn all the correct knobs in the correct way, and the bomb would simply find its way right into that old pickle barrel. "Simple" was surely the one thing this was not.

The Norden bombsight was highly classified. It was among a handful of really secret pieces of U.S. hardware. In addition to all the papers we'd filled out and the background checks we had patiently agreed to, there was an almost theatrical bit of business that became an integral part of our training routine. When it was time to actually use the bombsight, we would strap on a holstered sidearm, enter the bombsight vault, sign a special form, and march out to our airplane carrying a leather satchel containing the sight. I was never quite sure what I was expected to do if some foreign agent suddenly popped out from behind a No Parking sign and tried to grab my precious package. The pistol wasn't loaded so I couldn't even shoot him. In any case, this entire mickey-mouse procedure surely impressed on us how crucial the bombsight was to the war effort.

There was one problem with this clandestine exercise that was unknown to just about everyone. A year earlier, a U.S. bomber, equipped with a Norden bombsight, had landed in distress somewhere in Occupied France, and had been captured by the Germans. Although this misadventure must have been well known to Army Intelligence, (as always, an oxymoron) the word had not, during that year, filtered down to the rest of us. The bombsight in fact was treated with obsessive secrecy for many months to come. As it turned out, the Luftwaffe never bothered to build a comparable bombsight, possibly because they had too many other things to worry about.

There was also a melodramatic "Bombardier's Oath" that cadets were suppose to swear to, although I don't recall ever signing it. It went like this:

> "Mindful of the secret trust about to be placed in me by my Commander in Chief, the President of the United States, by whose direction I have been chosen for bombardier training . . . and mindful that I am to

> become guardian of one of my country's most priceless military assets, the American bombsight . . . I do here, in the presence of Almighty God, swear by the Bombardier's Code of Honor to keep inviolate the secrecy of any and all confidential information revealed to me, and further to uphold the honor and integrity of the Army Air Forces, if need be, with my life itself."

I suppose I should count it among my many blessings that such grave circumstances never occurred on my watch. I was never compelled to disclose the Secrets of the Bombsight to any enemy agent, although on a later occasion I did have to destroy one.

* * *

Inevitably, my acquaintanceship with Mr. Norden's bomb dropping machine blossomed into friendship. Practicing on some of the ingenious training equipment, my fingers would move everywhere at once, delicately adjusting, switching, turning, leveling—not unlike an accomplished organist. Mastering the bombsight, it turned out, was as much an art as it was a technical skill. And when we began to approach this virtuosity, we began to fly in real airplanes and drop real practice bombs.

Daytime missions started at first light. Another cadet and I would meet our instructor on the flight line, bundled up against the morning chill and armed with all the necessary impedimenta. Besides the aforementioned bombsight, this includes parachute and harness, flashlight, oxygen mask, a very heavy movie camera, computer, tachometer, stop watch, brief case, pencils, clip board, and, of course, lots of bulky flying clothes.

In the black dawn, it was usually necessary to walk around for many long minutes trying to find the airplane we were assigned to. Quite often, our bombs had not yet been loaded so we would then lift ten practice bombs up to the bomb bay, shackle them and place the arming wires on them. The practice bombs were long steel tubes painted blue and filled with sand. The nose was tapered and contained an impact fuse and just enough black powder to make an explosion visible from our bombing altitude. The back end had fins to give it the proper trajectory. It weighed exactly 100 pounds.

I would crawl up to the nose and crouch over the bombsight. I'd proceed through a complex pre-flight check of some twenty steps. My partner lounged in the rear. Later, he would open the camera hatch to film each drop. After five drops we'd change places. The pilot appeared and we tumbled out of the plane to salute him. We held a little conference to get our interphone signals straight. The instructor sat with the pilot, I joined my partner in the rear, the engines started up, and we took off.

If I was to bomb first I'd go forward and begin recording temperature, airspeed, altitude, etc. The other cadet would remove the pins from the ten bombs, thus arming them. At bombing altitude, we headed over the Mohave Desert towards the target range. I would begin the many computations with my instruments and feed them into the bombsight. Usually, I was too busy to look around, but after a few false alarms such as farms and small towns, I would see the target, a huge circle outlined on the desert floor.

I opened the bomb bay doors, switched on the Pilot Direction Indicator (PDI) and was now steering the plane. I would manipulate the many knobs of the bombsight like the maestro that at this point I was not. "Bombs away, sir!" I'd shout through my throat mike, knocking off my oxygen mask in the excitement. Then I'd wildly hit switches, readjust the sight, write down pertinent data, and look below for the impact. All this would occur in the 27.7 seconds it took the bomb to fall at this altitude. "A hit!" I would yell, (If indeed I were that lucky) and then we would turn for another run.

This entire procedure was repeated four more times and if everything worked, my average score for this mission should be below 230 feet—not exactly that proverbial pickle barrel. This referred to the Circular Error (CE) radius—the distance from the center of the target—and it was upon this number that my military future totally rested. To graduate, a bombardier required an average CE of less than 230 feet. I would be dropping hundreds of practice bombs over the next few months and oh so many bad things could happen—adverse weather, poor visibility, mechanical glitches, my own frailties—but nonetheless, I must average a CE of below 230 feet.

Next, I would crawl to the rear of the plane to let my partner drop his bombs. It was seriously cold back there. At 15,000 feet, with the bomb bays open, it could be a below zero wind chill. I would lean out of the camera hatch to get a shot of each bomb hit. Finally, the doors would be closed, we'd lose altitude, end our refrigeration, and head home. We landed, the pilot chewed us out by habit, and the mission was over. We returned to the Ready Room and would spend an hour filling out a dozen forms, some of impossible length, recording every detail of each of our five bomb drops. It was nearly supper time—it had been another hard day at the office.

Night bombing was an almost metaphysical experience, beautiful beyond belief. On those flights I had the feeling of complete separation from the earth. Above, the stars were plastered to the Plexiglas dome of the airplane and below, the lights of civilization were a vast ornamental garden. Our round lighted target looked like birthday candles on a black cake and when the bombs hit, there was a brief bright flash. But in spite of all this poetry, night bombing practice for neophyte bombardiers, was certainly more difficult.

The cross hairs in the bombsight and the leveling bubbles of the gyro were nearly invisible. There were no lights in the nose of the airplane and I could never find my many tools without a flashlight. Some of the switches and knobs were painted with fluorescent stuff which had a spooky appearance, but was of little help. And later, in the back of the plane, lying over the camera hatch taking movies in the icy wind and unable to see anything whatsoever, I'd begin to think more kindly about a job in the field artillery or even the infantry. So I'd spit down 15,000 feet, shrug my frozen shoulders, and figure things couldn?t get any worse.

We'd land and I would find I was wrong. I was scheduled to fly another mission. Finally, and after another hour of filling out forms, I would struggle, almost comatose, to the mess hall, and then to my blessed sack.

And so it went for many weeks—day bombing, night bombing, and ground school, punctuated by wild rides into L.A. and restless evenings looking for whiskeyish relaxation or compliant girls or something or other. What we were doing was pretty exciting, but the work was hard and the hours overfilled.

* * *

A long anticipated adventure during our last month at Victorville was to be a week of low altitude bombing in the Mohave Desert. We wore old khaki shirts and pants, and warm jackets. We were traveling light. There would be no spit and polish on this assignment, no hats, no salutes. We would eat from mess-kits, smoke, drink beer, never shave and seldom wash. It was a bivouac that for eight days would turn us into archetypal desert rats.

We arose every morning before dawn and didn't see the inside of our tents again until well after sundown. The nights were cold. I slept under three blankets, two comforters, and my fleece-lined flying clothes. We would fly either mornings or afternoons. When our flights were over, and after the usual hour of filling out forms, we would begin our various work details. K.P. was easy at a bivouac mess; guard duty at

3a.m. was bitter cold and I'd be sleepy, and why would a spy be out in the desert, anyway? We also had firing range practice—a few hundred rounds with pistol, carbine, tommygun, and of course, more time on the skeet range.

And then there was the bomb dump. On most days, when we weren't flying, we were unloading those 100 pounders from trucks, fusing them, reloading them onto small trailers, driving them out to the airstrip, and loading them into the airplanes. Our work details lasted about six hours and since each bomb was lifted four times, and since a thousand practice bombs were dropped each day, I calculated that I was personally heaving twenty tons on my shift. Towards the end, those suckers really got heavy.

We flew like mad—up to ten full missions a day. The idea was to not waste a minute of daylight flying time since our primitive airstrip had no lights. A plane would land and the gasoline and maintenance trucks would rush up to prepare it for the next mission. The bomb detail would load, shackle, and arm the ten bombs before the pilot could even get out to take a leak. The two cadets who had completed the mission would leap out and two new ones would take their place and the plane would taxi down the runway. We could fly five one-hour missions in less than six hours and our total bomb tonnage really showed it.

When we warriors returned to the formal garrison atmosphere of Victorville, it was a great scene. Back from the sagebrush and cactus, we arrived just as most of the cadet squadrons were marching to mess. It was Saturday and they were in their Class A uniforms. We climbed down from the trucks, sunburned, unwashed and unshaven, dressed as casually as can be imagined—many in dirty shorts—and we could feel their eyes upon us. We were the senior class and these other guys would someday be desert rats too. But for now, we must have looked pretty salty.

*   *   *

It was early April and we were on the last lap. Our flying exercises during this last week, were something new and quite exciting. We went to a briefing, just as we would someday in a real combat theatre. A huge map of Southern California was on the wall with a ribbon leading to the Initial Point (IP) and the target. The target might be the Hollywood Bowl, or the L.A. airport, or the Santa Anita racetrack, or whatever. Instead of bombs, of course, we carried cameras, but everything else was realistic. The idea was to give us some experience in orienting ourselves over large urban areas—generally considered to be the most difficult and confusing kind of landmark identification. We took turns navigating and camera bombing and it was exhilarating and a little scary to be over a vast city in a bomber. No one was shooting at us and there was no smoke or carnage below, but simply observing the vulnerability of Los Angeles was a sobering experience.

We also had a mission to drop some real bombs to give us an idea of what an actual explosion looked like. Instead of the 100 pound practice bombs which contained only a few pounds of black powder, we carefully loaded some high explosive demolition bombs and dropped them on a fake battleship in the desert. The effect was striking. They really did knock things about.

As far as handling these real bombs was concerned, we were taught that they were safer than the cheaply made practice bombs we'd caressed so carelessly and they were equipped with several redundant safety devices. They could, for example, be dropped thousands of feet without exploding if the fuse cotter pins were not removed. I suppose I should have been contemplating the terrible consequences these weapons begat—buildings destroyed, people killed—but somehow, such thoughts did not come to me then as they would later.

* * *

Finally, my navigator and bombardier training ended.

There was a parade of the entire cadet corps, and a somewhat forgettable graduation ceremony. When it was over, a guy named McCafferty and I pinned gold bars on each other's shoulders. I pinned on my silver wings myself. I was now an officer and a gentleman and after fourteen months of hope and effort, I felt wonderful.

Walking back to my barracks, I came upon a hurrying corporal. He snapped me a quick, almost perfunctory, salute and I grandly returned it. It was my first.

Second Lieutenant Alter, with his very shiny wings, climbed on the Super Chief for the two-day trip home. I was fully prepared to knock Chicago dead and a ten-day leave should be more than adequate.

The less said about those ten days, the better. Most of my men friends were serving Uncle Sam. Most of my women friends were away at college. After my many months of hyperactivity, there wasn't much to do. I was lonely and the weather was awful.

CHAPTER 11

I was soon on the Super Chief again and following my orders, reported to Hammer Field in Fresno, California. This was an AAF reception center where combat crews were quickly assembled from the thousands of pilots, bombardiers, navigators and gunners streaming in from the many specialty training fields. Each crew consisted of ten men who were almost always strangers to each other. It was a random draw for some significant future relationships. Thus, my crew, all ten of us, finally met, shook hands, and began to take each other's measure.

The pilot, who would be our bossman from this moment on, was First Lieutenant Everett Steiner from Kansas. (I never heard his first name used—he was always just "Steiner"). He was in his late twenties—an old man in AAF terms—and was the classic picture of what a veteran pilot should look like. He was square-jawed, high-spirited, and as we later learned, a talented lover. He was also a more experienced pilot than most of the other new crews had drawn. He'd logged well over a thousand hours as an instructor in Texas and this gave us an agreeable feeling of security. (Which, I should note, we never lost for the rest of the war.) Also of interest, was the fact that Steiner had been trained to fly B-24s. Ergo, that would be the airplane that we would fly.

Besides Steiner, the crew included Bill Rondeau, co-pilot, Al Hyman, navigator—both Second Lieutenants—and six sergeants. Early in the war, the Army had realized that the German prisons offered better living conditions to officers, including non-commissioned officers. Thus, all flying personnel were at least sergeants.

B-24 operational training was shared by five AAF fields in California and Nevada. Four of them were remote desert posts, far from any town that anyone could name. Our training would be through the summer months and desert temperatures soared to three digits every day. The fifth post was March Field near the pleasant town of Riverside and only an hour or so from L.A. Naturally, every new crew in the B-24 cadre, and there were many hundreds, thirsted for March Field.

Now it so happened, that Bill Kahn, an old friend of mine, was stationed at Hammer Field and that he, *mirabile dictu*, was a sergeant in the very office that made the training assignments for each crew. By the end of that week at Hammer Field, my crew and I were happily on our way to the Elysian Field of March.

* * *

Operational training was a melange of experiences. We were rehearsing for a war with real airplanes, real guns, and almost real combat situations.

Our training missions, which could last as long as six hours, were quite different from the ones I'd flown at Victorville. Instead of just giving practice to a couple of cadets, these long excursions were for the entire crew. We had to get used to working as a team and developing a lot of togetherness. So we flew and we flew and we flew. There was some cross-training. I already was a pretty good navigator and I continued to maintain logs on our daytime trips. Our engineer and our radioman learned a bit about each other's jobs. As designated Gunnery Officer, I supervised extra training for everyone at each gun position.

Most of our training was daytime. I was always busy preparing to bomb, bombing, or reporting the results of our bombing. Sometimes we would drop on desert targets, other times we'd camera bomb strategic buildings in L.A. and environs. Once, I scored a direct hit on Boulder Dam, and another time I wiped out a small town in Nevada called Las Vegas. We would often fly in close formation with other B-24s—important training for our pilots.

We would sometimes defend ourselves from attacking fighters using cameras mounted on our turrets. This was exciting . . . and very safe. We also had gunnery practice using live ammunition and firing at targets towed by B-26s. The crews of those tow planes must have fervently hoped that the tow-rope was long enough and that our gunners were proficient enough. The sound and vibration from ten 50 caliber machine guns was stunning.

We had our share of night missions. The sea at night was simply dark and forbidding, but L.A. from 20,000 feet was truly the City of Angels—a vast fairyland of millions of lights flickering in sync with the stars above us.

* * *

I was learning that a B-24 was one big mother—a vast and complex piece of machinery. It weighed over 18 tons empty and 32 tons fully loaded. It had a service ceiling of 28,000 feet, a range of 2100 miles, and a maximum speed of 290 mph. It was almost seventy feet long. It had miles of wiring, dozens of electric motors, hundreds of feet of hydraulic and oxygen tubing, several hundred light bulbs of various types, three completely separate radio sets, four or five independent systems for letting down the landing gear or opening the bomb bays or ditching the aircraft, over a hundred instruments in the cockpit, a small gasoline engine—called the putt-putt—for generating power on the ground when the main engines weren't running, and much, much more.

The four enormous (1200 hp) Pratt & Whitney engines gave the ship its power, but it could, and on occasion did, stay aloft with just two engines. While the Liberator was no longer the biggest or the fastest AAF bomber, it had the most safety features and the greatest redundancy. The hydraulics and electrical systems could be shot away, the control cables severed, two engines gone, and this bird would still fly.

It is interesting to note that while more B-24s were built than any other type bomber—nearly 20,000—today there is only one that is still flying. (There are a few non-operating B-24s in scattered aircraft museums.) This survivor flies around the U.S. and appears at airports and special exhibits to raise money so that it can continue flying around the U.S.

In 1998, over fifty years later, that lonely B-24 was exhibited at an airfield near Chicago. I showed my wife around the airplane and tried to explain everything. But when I tried to crawl through the tunnel to the bombardier's nose position or to squeeze through the bomb bay area, it was impossibly tight. Somehow, that B-24 had shrunk. (See page 150)

* * *

Although we usually used our open post passes in Riverside at the exotic and bizarre Mission Inn Hotel, we occasionally headed for Los Angeles. Here we sought out the late closing clubs and caroused our weekends away. Most of my memories of those L.A. trips are too blurred to recall.

One incident does stand out. A pilot named Liles and I

rented a car in L.A. one afternoon and just before we returned it the next morning, I nicked the fender as I was parking. The rental agency said they would send me a bill for the damage. Then, the day before we were ordered overseas, I got an invoice for some outrageous amount—it seemed enough to buy the entire car. Due to the press of more important matters, I decided to forget it.

At a mail call the following December at my bomber base in Italy, and after a harrowing mission where I'd once again faced my own lack of immortality, I opened a letter from the rental agency threatening legal action. Maybe, I thought, they could subpoena me back to California and wouldn't that be wonderful.

* * *

Our frequent contacts with the everyday world, especially there in Southern California, were instructive. The war was everywhere. The civilian portion of the Great American Pie in WW II was as committed as the military. Over 16 million men and women were under arms, a number that seems inconceivable today. But there were tens of millions of Americans not in uniform, and their patriotic fervor, as I think about it six decades later, seems even more extraordinary. While we soldiers were going through the paces I've been describing, what were all those other folks doing? They were building the greatest war machine the world had ever seen. They were manufacturing thousands of ships, and tens of thousands of airplanes, tanks, trucks, and cannon. They were supplying millions of shells, bombs, and bullets—not to mention the blankets, sun glasses, shoes, toothbrushes and jockstraps used by millions of fighting men.

The sheer magnitude was too staggering to contemplate. Never before in this world was so much stuff produced; never before was so much stuff needed; and perhaps, never again would such an immense output be possible. No one today under the age of seventy can possibly understand.

*   *   *

As the summer of 1944 wore on, the Southern California temperatures kept rising. We would move through our preflight procedures, for example, and it might be in the nineties. One day, while checking out something or other, I touched an upper section of our shiny aluminum fuselage and got such a bad burn that I had to report to the emergency medical hut for a bandage. You could have easily fried eggs on our wing—maybe even broiled a steak.

The weird part of this high temperature ordeal was that not too many minutes after takeoff, we would be miserably cold. We would board our aircraft practically stripped. At 5000 feet, we'd put on summer flying jumpers; at 10,000, we'd roll down our sleeves and hook up our oxygen masks; at 15,000 we were wearing jackets and gloves; and when we finally arrived at our operating altitude of 20,000 feet, we had pulled on heavy fleece-lined coats, trousers, boots and helmets and still we would shiver. Six hours later, we'd land under the afternoon sun, I would step out on the hardstand pouring perspiration, with my feet still frozen.

*   *   *

On the last weekend of our training program at March Field, about a dozen of us arranged for our grand finale at a hotel in Long Beach. Here was one of the great amusement parks of the country, dozens of glitzy hotels, and miles of wonderful beaches. We rode the world's tallest roller coaster over and over. We met girls. We checked out every bar in town. We met girls. We tanned our bodies for hours on the beach adjoining our hotel. We met girls. We were young flying officers enjoying our last fling before facing the enemy and perhaps a hero's death. In short, we were the answer to every maiden's prayer and we took every possible advantage of every maiden we could find.

We had booked several rooms and suites, stocked them with a cornucopia of liquids, and quickly filled them with a goodly number of enthusiastic young women. The drill was to sun oneself on the beach, meet a couple of girls also sunning, invite them up to our rapidly expanding party, and then go down to the beach and begin all over. We managed to keep this Bacchanalia alive for nearly three days until we had run out of liquor and money—but never girls.

It was a really magnificent ending to our many months of training.

CHAPTER 12

In early August, we arrived at Hamilton Field, just outside San Francisco. Over the next few days, we were exhaustively briefed for a post somewhere in the Pacific. We had complete physicals and were inoculated for every imaginable tropical disease to be found in the Pacific. We were issued hot weather clothing and equipment, including mosquito netting, canteens, insect repellent, malaria pills, and tons of other stuff for the Pacific.

At dawn on our last morning we got our final instructions and routings to Hickham Field in Hawaii, our first stop in the Pacific. We climbed into our brand new, very shiny B-24 and waited for the order to take off and meet our destiny in the Pacific. It was Pacific, Pacific, Pacific. Two hours later, we were called back to the Operations Room, told to turn in all of our tropical equipment, and were then bussed to a waiting train. Within a week, we would be on a ship, bound not for the Pacific, but for Europe.

I suppose all of this could be dismissed as simply another Army SNAFU (situation normal, all fucked up), but it was probably not that simple. The massive air war in Europe had been going on for over a year and hundreds of the surviving crews were finishing their tours of duty and being rotated home. The large pool of replacement crews—and that's what we were—was being quickly tapped. The European Theatre apparently maintained some degree of priority.

The railroad journey was forever—from San Francisco to Norfolk, Virginia was a long way under the best of conditions, and our conditions were only marginal. We added up to some forty crews, four hundred men, and since we'd been together for several months at March Field, we knew each other well. The trip once again turned out to be one continuous card game. After the porters made up our berths, we slept, but the rest of the time we played. The train had no diner so our meals were served at our seats and interrupted the games only briefly. I remember trying to deal a hand of five-card draw while I was slurping a bowl of hot cereal. I don't remember whether I won or lost during our long week in that Santa Fe Railroad casino.

Whenever the train stopped for fuel or supplies or simply for the sake of stopping, hundreds of us would try to climb down and stretch our legs. But armed MPs were always there to bar the way. We were on a so-called sealed train on a secret mission to a secret air field in a secret country. As usual, we didn't know where the hell we were going, but the Army seemed to be afraid that we might tell somebody.

* * *

Our port of embarkation was Fort Patrick Henry in Norfolk, Virginia—actually Hampton Roads—and it had an almost mystical overseas atmosphere that most U.S. posts lacked. Even though our every move seemed blanketed in secrecy, we could actually feel the tension in the inevitable question—where were we going from here?

Sooner, rather than later, we marched up the gangplank in that traditional scene from every wartime movie. Long lines of trudging men, Red Cross girls passing out coffee, cranes loading cargo, and all the hustle and bustle of an embarkation cliché.

* * *

Our ship was the Athos II, a Greek liner sailing with a French crew under U.S. Navy supervision, and part of a large convoy of dozens of cargo ships and several escorting destroyers. It was an old vessel, of medium size, and had been converted, rather badly, to a troop ship. On the upper decks were housed some 300 male officers and 600 nurses and USO and Red Cross women. Below decks—way below— were 2000 enlisted men stacked in bunks four high. There was a small lower stern deck where these poor guys, a few hundred at a time, could get some air and see the sun. Our own quarters were cramped, with a lot of us wedged into each cabin, but at least we weren't down in the hold. Strolling the upper decks was infinitely more pleasant and the gender ratio was extravagant.

The voyage was long—actually about four weeks. The ocean was blessedly calm so seasickness was minimal. We read a lot, played plenty of cards, and talked incessantly to each other. At night, there was some live entertainment, a few mediocre movies, but then, after a few evenings, a remarkable social ritual unfolded.

First there was the agreeable summer weather and the broad empty decks; then there was the reality of two women for each man and the inevitable urge of doing what comes naturally. And finally, because we were sailing in a convoy through hostile waters, there was the absolute certainty of a total blackout each night. Everyone knew that under no circumstances would anyone ever shine a flashlight in one's face, no matter what one was doing on deck. It was an ironclad guarantee. And the evenings were thus quite congenial.

* * *

Our ship also carried a few U.S. Navy officers who handled communications with the rest of the convoy and might also have had some secret duties I didn't know about. One afternoon, as I sat on deck perfecting my tan, I fell into conversation with an oldish Lieutenant, J.G. I happened to ask him why no one was manning the guns on the uppermost deck. There were two caliber.50 machine guns and a 105 mm cannon. The Navy guy said that no personnel had been assigned to operate them and that was too bad because someday we might see enemy subs or aircraft or whatever. I pointed out that there were several hundred trained aerial gunners on board who could certainly handle the 50s.

He was interested and after a day or two, I was invited to pick out some gunners and report back. We hustled a few of them up to the sun and air. Clearly, they were not unhappy to leave the dimly lit, and very stuffy, hold. We climbed to the uppermost deck and looked over the guns. There was no problem—they were identical to the ones we had all taken apart and fired so many times at gunnery school.

So a few of us took turns sitting in the sun on the upper deck, sometime gazing out to sea, but mostly looking down to the main deck where hundreds of neat looking girls, in a beguiling array of costumes, were sunning themselves. It was tough duty and as it turned out, we machine gun folks were never called upon professionally.

And so passed the weeks. There was one exciting submarine alert and we watched the tin cans (destroyers) zigzag around and through the convoy, but it was a false alarm. We finally steamed through the Straits of Gibraltar and as a rookie overseas traveler, I was fascinated by the thought of Europe on my left and Africa on my right. After a few days on the Med—I was picking up the lingo fast—we entered the harbor of Naples. The quotation "See Naples and die" popped into my head, but I thought it was inappropriate and sent it away. The harbor was, in fact, quite beautiful, and very, very busy. It was early September of 1944 and Allied ground forces, along with dozens of 15th Air Force groups were being supplied through these harbor facilities. Naples was also the headquarters of MTOUSA (Mediterranean Theatre of Operations, USA) which was sited at nearby Caserta.

* * *

We disembarked from our cocoon, Athos II, and marched through the unfamiliar streets of the Naples waterfront. This was my first foreign experience. Everything was different—the bombed-out buildings, the strange language, the strong smells, the pervasive squalor. We saw ill-clad, emaciated, wretched people. We heard ragged little boys running alongside us offering, in broken English, the sexual favors of their older sisters. This was the true debris of war. They were the innocent—not wicked, not arrogant, just utterly hapless. And who among us could not help but contrast these children with the kids we used to be, playing on the streets of our American cities?

At one point, as we marched along, a group of urchins ran alongside asking for money. Someone tossed them a few coins and apparently hoping for an authentic Italian song, perhaps even something operatic, asked if they would serenade us. The instant result was a wonderfully accented version of "Pistol Packin' Mama, Lay That Pistol Down" followed by "Home on the Range." Evidently, we were not the first Americans to have entered Naples.

We reached a railhead and entrained to our first foreign post. We rode on a typical continental train which chugged along so slowly that we could jump off and walk beside it. Each time it stopped in a village, we would be mobbed by people of all ages asking for cigarettes, money, candy, anything. At one point I traded someone a pack of Camels for a bottle of Marsala—a gross overpayment, I later learned, but the wine was great. Listening to the beautiful language was a treat, and the gestures were right out of Puccini.

One of the pilots in our crowd was an Italian-American, and he had taught us a number of helpful phrases for use in assorted situations—for example, when you wanted sex or conversely, when you didn't. As time went on, most of us learned enough idiomatic Italian—really street talk—to get along reasonably well. The first words we picked up, of course, were mostly obscene, but later we were able to buy food, receive directions, and even build a small hut with the few Italian words we knew blended with the few English words the natives knew.

* * *

Naturally, our first foreign post turned out to be a replacement depot. We would hang out here until our paperwork caught up with us and then some clerk would decide which combat unit needed us most. Daytime passes were easily available and we sallied forth to look for whatever delights still remained in Italy. Transportation was simply a matter of raising one's thumb to a passing truck or jeep, and since the roads were alive with military vehicles, we were able to explore a fair portion of the Campania region. We visited the vast and splendid palace in Caserta. We clambered over Roman remnants and walked around what was left of some of Il Duce's public works.

Early on, we changed our American money into lira. It was compulsory because the government obviously didn't want easily negotiable U.S. currency to fall into enemy hands. Although Italy was no longer considered the enemy, there were more than a few Italians around us whose sympathies were still with the Axis. Real lira were worthless and the American Military Government (AMG) had issued so-called invasion lira—acceptable to civilians and soldiers alike. The rate was one cent to one lira, so for my 120 bucks, I received 12,000 lira. I suddenly felt very rich, especially since a haircut was only fifteen lira and a glass of decent wine only ten. This was routine pricing, but for 2000 lira, I was also offered a battered ring that was green on the inside and had been made in Cleveland, Ohio.

* * *

After the allotted bureaucratic week in the hands of the Allied High Command, we were sent to another replacement depot near the town of Goia. About the only memory I have of this field is that on our first evening we had expected to go to the post's outdoor movie theater alongside the airstrip. An hour before the show started, while it was still light, a B-24 landed, blew a tire, and veered towards the theatre. One wing sheared the projection booth in two, the wheels crushed most of the seats, and the propellers chewed up the big screen. Later, a small sign was posted—there would be no movie that night.

Finally, after a reprise of all the forms we had already filled out, we scrambled into a war-weary B-24 and were flown to our new combat assignment. Now, after twenty months of active duty, I was about to participate in World War II.

CHAPTER 13

Our crew, always referred to as Steiner's crew, was now a member of the 780th Bombardment Squadron of the 465th Bombardment Group (Heavy) of the 55th Wing of the Fifteenth Air Force. We were over the mountains from Naples in Apulia, the southeastern region of Italy. We were an hour or so by jeep from Bari, a large port on the Adriatic, and we were somewhat closer to the town of Foggia. We were adjacent to a tiny village called Pantanella, and perched on a farm, which we'd been told, was owned by an Italian princess—a story that I've always wanted to believe was true.

Some months earlier, ground personnel of the 465th had laid the mile long steel runway strips, pitched dozens of pyramidal tents and built mess halls, operation headquarters and other necessary structures. The two airstrips and the maintenance buildings were in a large valley, but our tents and all the facilities for everyday living were on a hill overlooking that valley. It had proved to be a very functional, and almost agreeable, site. The view was especially fine.

We were among the first of the replacement crews to arrive. Because of the good flying weather during the summer of 1944, many of the original crews were finishing up their required number of missions and new blood (!) was needed. By the time our crew showed up, the squadron had flown eighty-one accredited missions, and had seen eleven planes—carrying 110 men—shot down.

Our first evening in the friendly confines of the 780th was instructive. We were shown around the place and ended up at the recently built officers' club for some cherry brandy—one of the few drinks available at this post. Then to dinner in the mess hall and introductions to most of the other officers in the squadron. And then, with a few winks and nudges, we were escorted to the operations tent for the nightly broadcast of the infamous Axis Sally. The program, which the old timers had heard many times, was naturally heavy with propaganda about the glorious victories of the Third Reich and larded with misinformation about how many U.S. airplanes had been shot down by heroic Luftwaffe pilots and intrepid antiaircraft gunners.

Finally, came the climax of the evening. "We would like to welcome," said Sally in her soft and beguiling voice, "The new arrivals to several of the Fifteenth Air Force groups." She therein rattled off a dozen squadrons by number and new crews by name. Included was, "And we welcome Steiner's crew to the 780th." We were, to put it mildly, stunned.

It had become such a regular occurrence that the squadron veterans were no longer troubled by these insolent broadcasts. With dozens of Italian laborers working within the squadron area, it would have been odd not to have chanced upon some serious spying. The bottom line, however, was that the vaunted German intelligence machine was able to uncover information about almost everything going on inside our squadron premises—everything, that is, except the target of tomorrow's mission. And that, of course, was all they really wanted to know.

Not long after this brush with Nazi intimidation I was assigned one evening to join what can only be described as a posse. It seemed that someone in our Group had either seen, or had met someone who had seen, a suspicious vehicle, or maybe just a suspicious pedestrian, on one of our military roads. It was that vague. Accordingly, a number of armed officers were dispatched in jeeps to patrol the roads. Exactly what we were looking for was never fully explained, and after several hours of aimlessly driving around, we returned to our units and the matter was never mentioned again.

* * *

A tour of duty for an air crew, when I arrived, was fifty missions. This was computed by designating the easy ones—called milk runs—as singles, and the long, terrifying flights into Germany or Austria, as doubles. Later on, the task of sorting out these missions must have become too complicated, or perhaps too political, and then every sortie was simply counted as one. The tinkering did not end there. Our crew was first expected to fly twenty-five actual missions, and about the time I reached twenty-two, all tours were extended to thirty. And naturally, just as I approached the magic thirty, someone, maybe in Washington, raised it to thirty-five. The war ended before the required number could be increased again and I wound up with thirty-one.

Although Joseph Heller had not yet written *Catch 22*, the military mindset that created this disagreeable math, could have been straight out of that celebrated book.

The 465th Group had been activated a year earlier with four squadrons, including ours. The group had done most of its training in Nebraska, spent some time in North Africa, and had become operational in Italy in May of 1944.

Our crew, along with a half-dozen others, had arrived as the pleasant summer weather was changing into what would turn out to be an unusually cold and rainy winter. Not only would our required missions be stretched out for many months (the original crews had taken just four months to complete their missions, and most of us wouldn't be finished after eight) but all of us in the Group would have to do something about facing the winter.

* * *

What that something turned out to be was a fascinating example of good old Yankee resourcefulness. There was a tuffa rock (a porous limestone) quarry nearby and throngs of jobless Italian laborers available. For a few cartons of cigarettes, they would eagerly, and not inexpertly, build houses for us. These huts consisted of four stone walls, but since there was virtually no lumber anywhere, we had to make do with our pyramidal tents for roofs. This not only defined the shape and size of the house, but also gave it a rather curious architectural profile. For windows, we used Plexiglas from wrecked B-24s, offering a precious bit of daylight.

At night we had a single 40 watt light bulb at the top of our center pole. This low tech electric system, requiring more elaborate wiring than a nuclear reactor, was powered by a camp generator which offered little voltage and even less dependability. Our furnishings were Spartan but serviceable. GI cots, ammo chests for storage, steel bomb crates for stools, and a couple of woven mats on the floor. An old wing tank, placed outside and uphill, was piped in for running water. We even had a mouse and a tiny lizard. And, of course, we displayed the obligatory pinups of Betty Grable, Rita Hayworth, and Hedy Lamarr in a variety of revealing costumes. They were the official idols to whom we paid homage.

Our heat that cold winter came from another old tank that was mounted outside our hut, and since there was no kerosene available, we filled it with high octane aviation gas which then flowed through pieces of oxygen tubing and dripped into a small metal can. This "furnace" gave us a sub-standard, barely acceptable level of comfort. Because the flame would sometimes be blown out by the wind, and because the gas could drip all night, someone half-asleep the next morning, might throw a match into the can. The result was total incineration—of the huts, and on at least one occasion, the tenants.

* * *

As with all new crews, we were dispatched on a series of training missions, relearning everything that the brass thought we might have forgotten. We became familiar with our home field and its general neighborhood. This would be particularly important on those occasions when we returned from a long mission with only a spoonful of gas. We also were rounded up for more ground school sessions and fed operational advice specific to the habits of the local Luftwaffe.

CHAPTER 14

Our practice missions ended and we were now eligible, and foolishly impatient, for our first combat mission. I was excited. I was resolute. I was Henry the Fifth, Ethan Allen, and Phil Sheridan anticipating my next battle. But even after long, interrogative dialogues with the veterans of our squadron, I had absolutely no concept of what was awaiting us.

The drama of these missions actually began the night before. We would hurry over to the Squadron Operations tent after chow. There, on a huge blackboard would be written the order of battle for the next day or, as was often the case that winter, we'd be told that the mission had been scrubbed. The names of the crewmen assigned to fly on that mission, along with the numbers of their assigned aircraft, were clearly noted. The bomb load was specified, but our destination was conspicuously absent. It was an anxious time, standing in the Operations tent and reading the white chalk letters on the blackboard. Our lives hung on those orders and we were always of two minds about it. On the one hand, most of us were not in a hurry to be shot at. On the other hand, we wanted to fly our missions, complete our tour of duty, and get the hell home.

So, on the evening of September 19, 1944, it was finally show time. My name appeared in white chalk letters on the blackboard that was like a marquee, in the operations tent that was like a stage. I was being cast in this play as a bombardier. To me, it was the major role. Never mind the pilot and the rest of the crew. They were simply backup. Never mind the seven other crews—they were just extras. This would be the production of my life.

In reality, I'd been named as bombardier for another crew also flying its first mission. My own crew was scheduled to fly without a bombardier. As was becoming customary, the navigator would simply toggle the bombs out when he saw the squadron leader drop his. I, however, was assigned to get some real time practice in actual bombardiering by setting up the bombsight and focusing on a target. The fact that it would be covered with smoke, dust, and bursting bombs, was the realism part.

Also becoming customary, was the random dividing of crews that until recently, had always been together. The AAF had decided that individual crew members could be assigned wherever needed and at the convenience of their commanders. Thus, we might fill in for someone who was sick, on leave, or simply needed elsewhere. In my case, I flew with Steiner on fewer than half of my missions.

* * *

We hurried back to our tent, laid out our gear and hit the sack early. While we slept, the work of preparing for the next day's mission was moving apace. Down on the flight line the mechanics were running up the engines and checking out the ten thousand things that could affect our future health and happiness. The radio guys were testing all the communication systems. The armorers were preparing the guns and the bombs. And at Group headquarters, the S-2 officers and Operations folks were planning every detail of the mission.

At 4:00 a.m. we were awakened by the heavy hand of the Charge of Quarters (CQ). "Briefing in 45 minutes," he shouted. It was totally dark and very cold, although it would get much colder as winter settled in. I dressed as quickly as I could. I had a slight case of the shakes. Over my cotton drawers went long woolen underwear. Then, my woolen winter uniform shirt and trousers. We always flew in uniform, with full insignia, so that if we had to parachute down, we wouldn't be shot as spies. On my feet were electrically heated cloth booties under insulated flight boots. I put on the newly issued heavy nylon flight jacket with some kind of fleecy lining. It took the place of the old sheepskin-lined leather jackets that were so difficult to move around in. Lastly, I stuffed my electrically heated jumpsuit, helmet and goggles, .45 caliber pistol, oxygen mask, parachute harness, and inflatable life jacket into my flight bag.

We ambled down the hill to the mess hall for what was invariably an unsatisfactory breakfast—partly because we were so nervous and partly because the food was pretty gross. Powdered scrambled eggs and shit-on-a-shingle, a special manifestation of Spam, was the cuisine of choice.

We hustled over to Group headquarters. There were a hundred officers seated in the briefing room. The air was heavy with cigarette smoke—nearly everyone smoked in those days and considering the kind of work we were doing, no one would have worried much about lung cancer, even if we had known about it. What we did know was that Chesterfields satisfied; we'd walk a mile for a Camel; and that just like us, Lucky Strike Green had gone to war. And whatever the brand, we would light up our cigarette with a Zippo.

We sat waiting and we gloomily tried to guess where today's mission would be pointed. At the front of the briefing room was a stage and an enormous map of central Europe, covered for the moment by a cloth curtain.

Suddenly, the Group Commanding Officer (CO) strode down the center aisle. "Tenhut!" someone shouted and we all stood up. "At ease." said the colonel and we all sat down. He mounted the stage, uttered a few introductory and encouraging words about how vital this mission was to the war effort. He gestured, the curtain was lifted and everyone took a deep breath. There on the map was a thick red string revealing the route of the day's mission. If the string ran northwestward to Munich, or northeastward to Vienna, or to any of a dozen other cruel targets, there would be a prolonged and thunderous groan. But this time the line went to Hatvan, Hungary, and from the general sigh of unmistakable relief, it seemed to be a milk run.

The briefing continued. The Group Operations Officer described the route and the target. We would zigzag over Yugoslavia avoiding known anti-aircraft positions and head into Hungary to hit the railroad marshalling yards in the small town of Hatvan. The flight would be long, but should be quite safe. The Intelligence Officer (S-2) told us that the target was a stretch for German fighter planes and that we should see only light flak. (On later missions, such as Regensburg or Bratislava, the S2 officer might note that the flak was HIA—heavy, intense, and accurate.) Photographs of the target area were projected on a screen. The Group Meteorologist gave us the word on the weather over Europe and the Adriatic. S2 also discussed escape routes in case we might have to parachute or crash land. Everyone knew, of course, that the chances of escaping capture this deep in enemy territory were between slim and non-existent.

We were issued escape kits which included a land map of the area where we would be, a hundred dollars in U.S.

currency, a tiny compass disguised to look like a button, a card with some foreign phrases, and other useful odds and ends. We're under strict orders not to carry any personal items that might give information to the enemy. If captured, we were to offer only our name, rank, and serial number.

An extreme example of a detailed briefing: While preparing for a mission to Vienna some months later, we were told that if we landed within the city, we should take a number 18 streetcar to the end of the line where resistance people would meet us. It was never fully explained how guys in flying clothes and American uniforms could board a Vienna streetcar.

So that everyone would have the same time on his watch, we set them, pulled out the stem, an operations officer said "Hack," and we restarted them. There was a short prayer by the chaplain and another encouraging word from the colonel. Bombsight settings, fusing information and navigational maps were passed out.

We left Group Headquarters and climbed onto one of the trucks waiting outside. We headed down the hill to the flight line and stopped at each hardstand on which an airplane was parked. The planes were widely dispersed in case of a German bombing attack. There was a good deal of kidding. At the first hardstand, as the crew climbed off the truck, one guy grabbed the railing and yelled, "I'm too young to die—I'm not going." I assumed he was just trying to be funny.

* * *

The truck pulled up to my assigned airplane. The name painted on the nose was "Portland Rose" and we had been told that this ship had flown many missions and been shot up a number of times. The air was cold and it was still pretty dark. We had nearly an hour before we would start our engines. We stowed our flight bags and began the lengthy preflight procedures. The pilot and copilot mounted the flight deck and started hitting switches and turning knobs. They had a long check list of things they must do. The navigator studied his maps by flashlight.

As gunnery officer, I checked the six gun positions with each of our six gunners. We made sure there was enough ammunition stored where it was supposed to be. We rotated the electric turrets, tried out the optical gun sights, and inspected the mechanical action of the guns. These were caliber .50 heavy machine guns and there were ten of them on board and thousands of rounds of ammo. I checked out the nose turret, the top turret, the two waist positions, the underneath ball turret, and the tail turret.

Next, I climbed into the bomb bays and closely examined the bombs and fuses. We were carrying eight five-hundred pound demolition bombs, fused to detonate on contact with the ground. There was a cotter pin inserted in each fuse which would prevent the bomb from accidentally exploding until I wanted it to. Later, I would arm them by removing the cotter pins.

My last visit was to my "office" in the nose of the B-24. Here, as usual, was the sacred and supposedly secret Norden bombsight. Nowadays, when I think about that bombsight, I'm astonished that it did so many things that a computer would someday do. It was a technological achievement almost magical for its time. It was not, however, nearly as effective as its press coverage. "Precision bombing" was mostly an oxymoron.

I ran some checks on the bombsight and the gyroscopes, shut them down and joined the rest of the crew and several mechanics out on the hardstand for a cigarette and an uneasy wait for takeoff. I was very nervous. The eastern sky was brightening, but there was a heavy overcast and we wondered if we'd really fly our first mission or see it scrubbed by the weather. This interlude, after finishing our preflight checks, but before takeoff, was always a tense time. I was learning that waiting around is not easy when one is as apprehensive as I seemed to be. Suddenly, two green flares soared into the sky above the control tower. The mission was on.

We scurried aboard our airplane. My takeoff position was on the floor of the flight deck. The rest of the guys scattered, sitting wherever they were comfortable. Except for the pilots, there were no seat belts. The pilot pushed the starter button for the first engine and it whined a few seconds, caught, and after being fed a rich mixture of high octane gas, it roared into life. The procedure was repeated for the other three engines, and as they joined the chorus, the airplane shook a bit, and we were in business. The pilots finished their other preflight steps. More flares from the tower. The ground guys pulled away our wheel chocks, and we began to roll along the tarmac.

There were nearly thirty big-assed birds lumbering in single file. There was Jackpine Job and Old Dutch Cleanser and Agony Wagon and Whiskey Jim and Alley Oop and we pulled in right behind Destiny's Tot. We lined up at the ends of the two steel-matted runways. The last flares were fired and the Group leaders began to pick up speed. The airplanes would be taking off just a few seconds apart. All thirty of the Group would be airborne in under two minutes. Our 780th would be the second squadron in the air and our plane was in number four position. When we were fully airborne, a typical squadron formation—called a box—would usually include seven aircraft.

It was our turn and we began to move onto the runway. The pilot set his brakes, pushed the four throttles as far forward as possible, released the brakes and we lunged ahead. The ship started to pick up speed. The engineer was standing between the two pilot seats watching the engine instruments. The copilot was calling off numbers on the airspeed indicator. At a certain speed, depending on the wind and other factors, the pilot would pull back on his control yoke and we'd be airborne. The very end of the runway would flash by at almost the same moment.

We were carrying 4000 pounds of bombs and 21,000 pounds of gasoline (2700 gallons), plus machine guns, ammo, and people. The total load was over thirty tons so it's no wonder we would sweat out the takeoff. There are two particularly important things the pilot must fret about. First, is the invisible point on the runway where he is irrevocably committed to keep going—where it's simply too late to change his mind. Second, is sensing the exact, the optimal, the perfect speed at which the plane will lift off without stalling, and yet not overrun the airstrip and plow into the fences at the end. In other words, the pilot must play this game like a master to prevent us from becoming an AAF statistic.

The co-pilot dealt with the landing gear and the flaps and we were underway. We immediately found ourselves in heavy clouds and we climbed for a long time without being able to see anything in the impenetrable soup—sometimes not even our own wingtips. Rain splashed over our windows. We bounced around in some unseen aircraft's prop wash. I spent my time wondering what the odds were of avoiding a collision with another airplane in this awful murk. Not good, I thought.

Hundreds of huge bombers were climbing through thick clouds without radar, ground control, or even radio contact. Nowadays, this would be considered utter madness. Friendly skies, indeed!

* * *

Suddenly, at perhaps 7000 feet, we were out of the gloom and it was a beautiful sun-filled, blue sky kind of day. Below us was solid undercast. Our squadron began to pull itself together and within a few minutes our seven planes were in their assigned box. We tried to maintain a tight formation to present as formidable a defense against enemy attack as possible. The wings of each aircraft nearly overlapped.

Looking around, we saw dozens of other airplanes trying to find their own squadrons. This mission was not planned as a maximum effort but there were still six groups assembling to make up the 55th Wing. That of course, added up to nearly 200 airplanes, 400 tons of bombs and 2000 heavy machine guns. Far above us and not visible, was our fighter escort—several squadrons of P-51s, usually referred to as our "Little Friends." One of them, as it happened, was the only all black fighter squadron to fly in WW II—the Tuskegee Airmen—and we loved them.

Climbing steadily, the squadrons were gradually joining their groups. To help them assemble, the B-24s of each Group had brightly colored, easily identifiable insignia painted on their twin rudders. Later, when the entire wing was spread out over several square miles of sky, it was awesome. I couldn't help but think how frightening it must look to the people down below who were at the wrong end of our hundreds of demolition bombs.

At 10,000 feet, the pilot told us it was oxygen time. I headed forward to my tiny bombardier compartment. On many later missions I would also be the navigator, but today there are three of us in the nose—the nose gunner cloistered in his turret, the navigator who had been filling in his charts since takeoff, and me.

I hooked up all of my umbilical cords. There was the hose through which oxygen flows from a central system to my mask. There was the radio line that connected my throat microphone and earphones to the plane's intercom. There was the electric cord that kept my suit and socks somewhat heated. My parachute chestpack was close by so I could quickly snap it to my harness in case of trouble.

The parachute harness went over my Mae West. (For younger readers, the Mae West life jacket—quite similar to those on today's commercial jets—was, when inflated, suggestive of a very chesty movie actress, for whom it was named.) I would put on my flak suit later, when we got over enemy territory. It consisted of small overlapping steel plates sewn into a sort of apron-vest. I also had a steel helmet.

So there I sat like a science fiction character. Everything was plugged in, everything was pretty important, and everything was uncomfortable.

And then there were all my bombardier tools—the E6B so-called computer, pads of paper, pencils, charts of many kinds, a stopwatch. I also had a movie camera to use after our bombs were released.

* * *

We were over the Adriatic Sea, which, as the undercast slowly broke up, was today a lovely shade of green. We were approaching Yugoslavia and our altitude was a cold 20,000 feet. It is worth pointing out that a B-24 was not equipped with heaters, and seemed to have more than its share of openings for icy drafts. We crossed the Dalmatian Coast into northwestern Yugoslavia, and we were now over Croatia, an ally of the Nazis and presently saturated with German military units. On our maps, the known installations of enemy anti-aircraft batteries were marked with red circles and we zigzagged to avoid them. This, of course, didn't help us to avoid the unmarked guns.

From the time of our takeoff until the time when I must prepare for my role as a working bombardier, would take four or five hours. I was a typical commuter with a long ride before I got to my job. The pilots were busy flying, the navigator was busy navigating and the six gunners were busy watching for enemy fighters. I, on the other hand, had a large block of unscheduled time. This was not an appropriate moment to read a book so I listened to Tommy Dorsey on Armed Forces Radio. I cracked jokes over the intercom. But mostly, I shivered.

We continued heading northeast over Yugoslavia. On the intercom a gunner shouted, "Flak at nine o'clock." Sure enough, I looked to my left and just a few miles north were the first puffs of flak I'd ever seen. I need not add that they wouldn't be the last. The guns were too far away to be of any concern, and the flak seemed as harmless as the blowing dust it resembled. We were now at 24,000 feet and it was really cold. The electric suit and all the other stuff I was wearing naturally helped, but unhappily, not enough. The wires in my left bootie must have shorted and I couldn't feel my toes.

I suddenly remembered last summer at Maxwell Field and how we suffered from the Alabama heat, and how the upperclassmen bellowed, "Mister, stop sweating!"

* * *

Since I've often been asked about it, perhaps a delicate word here on—ah—bodily functions. With all the layers of clothing we were wearing and with our inflexible attachments to oxygen, intercom, etc., the circumstances were difficult. Most of the guys simply peed into the bomb bays. The urine froze immediately and when the bomb bay doors opened over the target, our 500 pound bombs were accompanied by some yellow ice. Bowels presented a more complex dilemma. It was cold and we were scared and at 25,000 feet the outward pressure in our gut was painful. We were filled with angst and shit. There were few options and undressing was seldom one of them—at least not at high altitude. Hence, we must either stoically hold everything in, or expect to do some extra laundry when we got home. All things considered, however, this was not one of our major problems.

CHAPTER 15

We had been flying for over four hours and were now crossing into Hungary, still dodging German flak locations. It was time for me to arm the bombs. This was routinely done over enemy territory so that in case of a premature drop, our bombs might still do some tactical damage. I disconnected my electric suit cord and my intercom. I plugged my oxygen mask into a walk-around bottle—a container about the size of a small fire extinguisher that allowed me to wander about for a generous five or six minutes. At this altitude, I would live less than a minute without oxygen.

I hurried aft, crawling through the tunnel from the nose and then squeezing upright through the bomb bay. The bomb bay doors were closed, but on some later missions I would make this journey with the doors open, gazing down at the five miles of empty space between me and the good earth. I could not wear my parachute because it was impossible to squeeze one into this space. I was not connected to the intercom. I was feeling very much alone. I pulled out the cotter pins from the eight bomb fuses with pliers. The bombs were now ready to go to work—only on the target, I hoped.

I squeezed my way back to the nose. I reconnected all my lines again and prepared to do the job that the Army, at vast taxpayer expense, had trained me for.

I loaded fresh data into the bombsight—temperature, altitude, airspeed, etc. I crouched down, often simply kneeling. I made myself comfortable as best I could. The navigator shouted that we were ten minutes from the IP which gave me ten more minutes of anxiety. The IP is the Initial Point, the spot on the map where we turn toward the target and begin our actual bomb run. This may take six or eight or even ten minutes and is the period in which the bombardier locks his bombsight on the target, does his mysterious work and releases his bombs.

The bomb run is also that terrifying interval during which the German anti-aircraft gunners learned exactly what heading we were on, at what altitude we were flying, and what our airspeed was. Furthermore, they knew that we would make no changes for several long minutes. This gave them a splendid opportunity to fix their guns at the optimal settings to blow us away.

During this static maneuver—static on our part, not the enemy's—the only active defense we have is to throw out large quantities of something called "chaff" or "window." This was a finely shredded metal foil, similar to the stuff we toss onto our Christmas trees at home. As the generous handfuls of chaff fall below and behind our ship, the enemy radar is presumably misled about our altitude and heading, and their aim is accordingly spoiled. That's the theory we're told, but on this mission it doesn't seem to be doing a whole lot of good. It does, however, give our gunners something positive to do.

* * *

At last, we turned on the IP and over the intercom I heard the pilot say, "Alter, it's all yours." What he meant was that he had switched on the C-1 autopilot and through a remote mechanism called the pilot directional indicator (PDI), I was now controlling the direction of the aircraft. Looking through the viewfinder of my bombsight, I tried to do two critical things at the same time.

First, by guiding the airplane, I kept it on course and headed directly towards the target. If the vertical crosshair moved to the left or right, I made ever so slight adjustments with my left hand on the turn and drift knob. Then, as the target got nearer, I tried to place the bombsight's horizontal crosshair on the spot at which I was aiming, and with my right hand I delicately turned the rate knob to lock the crosshair at that point.

For some technical reason, both knobs are on the right side of the bombsight so I awkwardly crossed my left arm over my chest. At the same time, with my third hand, I adjusted the gyroscope knobs to keep the bombsight level. And with my fourth hand, of course, I pushed the lever to open the bomb bay doors.

If everything worked—the data I'd fed in, the sight leveling, the crosshair rate and the PDI control, my bombs would automatically release at exactly the right moment and go exactly where they were supposed to go. Dream on. It seldom happened because there were far too many variables and machines were just machines and I was just a human.

An example often cited regarding the accuracy of aerial bombardment involved a mission during the Blitz of London by the German air force. Records tell us that only half of their bombs even fell on England, not to mention London, and the rest plunged into the Channel. In WW II, for both sides, accurate bombing was mostly an aspiration. An RAF pilot once pointed out that the Allied air forces had made countless assaults on German agriculture.

Another part of the precision problem was the typical opacity of the target area covered as it was by smoke and debris from the bombs dropped by the squadrons ahead of us. It made aiming the bombs more difficult and determining the results of the drop more complicated.

But in spite of all of this grumbling about target exactness, U.S. and British strategic bombing was certainly impressive. By the end of the war, the mighty German industrial machine had been virtually destroyed. What our air forces lacked in precision, we unquestionably made up for in sheer bomb tonnage, aircraft production, and tens of thousands of trained personnel.

* * *

Back to the mission. Through all of this intense and disciplined activity of mine—this professional concentration—there was something else going on. The Germans were shooting at us. They were just as serious about this war as we were.

As my crosshairs passed the release point, we felt a sudden buoyancy in our airplane. I shouted "Bombs Away," and the pilot racked the now much lighter B-24 into a tight turn and with the rest of the squadron, began the evasive action we were not able to do before. It was my first chance to look around at the black, remarkably evil looking bursts of flak.

As has often been noted, the flak over a well protected target seems thick enough to walk on. Sometimes the burst was so close that we could see the bright red center of the explosion. Each furious burst, I tried not to remind myself, was a large steel projectile erupting into hundreds of angry fragments that traveled at blinding speed. We were trapped inside an aluminum tube, shielded by a skin only a few millimeters thick. In spite of the partial protection of my flak suit, I was painfully aware there was no place to hide. I kept my hands on my parachute chest pack. I persistently peeked at the nose wheel doors which were my only means of escape. I was, needless to say, frightened.

If this mission to Hatvan was a milk run, I was not looking

forward to those mornings when everyone groans as they hear that the target will be Vienna. As things turned out, this had not been such a terrible mission. What my unpracticed eye saw as a sky full of flak, the old timers regarded as merely light and inaccurate, and we had encountered no German fighter resistance.

* * *

But now we were pointing towards home, much lighter, and heading downhill—losing lots of altitude—and going much faster. After six hours in the air, we were less than two hours from Italy. When we reached 10,000 feet, we removed our chafing oxygen masks. I lighted my first cigarette in several hours. I opened a K Ration box and had some cheese and crackers, threw away some unidentifiable canned stuff, and then devoured a concentrated chocolate bar. The intercom came alive with jabber. Everyone was talking at once—excitement after our first mission, relief that we were all still alive, and the joy of a weight being lifted.

> Tail gunner to bombardier: "You got
> a direct hit, sir. I saw it all."
> The truth was, he saw practically
> nothing because of the smoke.
>
> Engineer to everyone: "That flak wasn't so bad."
> Waist gunner to engineer: "How the hell
> do you know? It's your first frigging mission."
>
> Pilot to everyone: "Okay you guys.
> Settle down and keep you eyes peeled
> for fighters."

We cruised through Yugoslavia again, dodged the flak circles, crossed the Adriatic, found our Pantanella airfield and landed. We unloaded our gear, climbed out of the airplane, and some of us patted the ground. We looked over the ship for flak damage, and there was little. Our squadron Flight Surgeon pulled up in a jeep and offered each of us a shot of whiskey—a local custom. We could also save up those shots and after so many missions, we'd be given a full bottle. I so elected. A truck stopped and we climbed on and headed back to Group Headquarters for interrogation in the same big briefing room.

Our crew sat down with an S2 officer who asked questions about the mission—the enemy presence, the intensity of the flak, and how our bombing pattern looked. Tonight, they would examine the aerial photos of the target area and have a better idea of how well we did. Since each of the crew had a different seat for the show, each was questioned about what he saw, and as with eye witnesses to almost any climactic event, each of us seemed to have seen some things differently.

After dinner, I stopped at the Operations tent to see if I was on the blackboard for tomorrow's mission. I wasn't. Some of the other guys moved on to the Officers Club to play cards or just drink, but I was too tired. Flying a combat mission turned out to be pretty hard work.

Our mission to Hungary on that September day was declared successful. We seriously damaged the Nazi marshalling yards and disrupted their freight traffic, at least for a while.

A year or so later, back in Chicago, my eighty-year old Hungarian grandmother told me she thought that some of my late grandfather's family might have come from Hatvan.

CHAPTER 16

Our next mission was to Munich and very rough. I was beginning to learn that the bigger German cities not only contained more of the strategic targets that invited our attention, but also boasted a vastly increased cover of anti-aircraft guns. The pattern of our missions was also becoming fairly fixed. Six to eight hours of bone chilling cold and uneasy expectation, climaxed by a few minutes of sheer terror. Except for the occasional milk run, this was to be my lot for thirty-one missions.

On the way home from this sortie to Munich, we were attacked by some ME-109 German fighters. Excited "clock" calls resounded on our intercom. "Fighter at 12 o'clock." "Two fighters at 3 o'clock." There was a lot of machine gun noise, but somehow the action was short lived and neither side seemed to have suffered any damage.

An excerpt from the book *Bomber Command* by Jeffrey Ethell, published after the war, is appropriate here. "Of all the combat jobs in the American service during WW II, from infantryman to submariner, no job was more dangerous, statistically, than that of a man in a bomber over Germany. The Eighth and the Fifteenth Air Forces took a higher percentage of losses than any other American fighting force, from foxhole to destroyer deck...."

Postwar statistics have shown that for all theaters of operation, over 22,000 Allied bombers were shot down and 110,000 airmen died. During the worst of the Eighth Air Force bomber strikes in England in late 1943, the average life of a bomber crew was fifteen missions. And for an extreme example, on the infamous Schweinfurt/Regensburg raid, 315 B-17s took off, 60 were shot down, 17 were scrapped, and 121 needed major repairs—total: 198.

For us during that autumn of 1944, the truth was that the mighty Luftwaffe was nearly defanged. Once the most powerful air force in the world, it had come upon hard times. American and British bombers had repeatedly shattered the German aircraft factories. (I flew on several such missions.) They would be rebuilt and then bombed again. It was not easy to produce high quality airplanes under such conditions. The oil fields and refineries of the Third Reich had also been ravaged over and over again, leading to serious aviation fuel problems.

Most calamitous, was the attrition of the pool of qualified German pilots. Our fighter planes and well-armed bombers had shot down thousands of German aircraft. The planes could slowly be replaced, but not the guys who flew them. At this moment in 1944, the Luftwaffe was deploying kids with a few months of training against Americans with nearly two years. It was no contest. This was the good news.

The bad news was that as the American armies pushed eastward and the Soviet military machine pushed westward, the German cannon—primarily the fearsome and very mobile 88s—were also being moved eastward and westward. By winter, there were more anti-aircraft guns squeezed around our major targets than anyone could have envisioned. Their density per acre was too terrible to even think about. Most aircrews dreaded flack even more than German fighter planes because they could only sit in their aluminum tubes and helplessly watch it. There was no way of fighting back.

* * *

We had an easy mission to Athens—easy in the sense that the distance was shorter and the flak was more moderate. Our target was a marshalling yard complex north of Piraeus and we were a smaller attack force than usual. We were high and it was hazy, but I did get a quick glimpse of the Acropolis as we made our turn onto the IP. It was far behind us when the thought came to me about how awful some bombardier would feel if he had added to the desecration of the Ottoman Turks by accidentally blowing up a piece of the Parthenon.

On this mission, we had a bomb hang up in the bomb bay. For no apparent reason, when I toggled out our load, this one guy simply wouldn't drop. It was an awful experience. We couldn't possibly land with a hung up bomb because it might explode just as we touched down. Someone had to dislodge it, and that was naturally the bombardier's job. I squeezed myself back to the bomb bay. The doors were open and the ground was perhaps four miles straight down. This was not one of my better moments. I was standing, without my parachute, on a foot wide catwalk with my arm wrapped tightly around one of the supporting stanchions.

The shackle of a 500 pounder was jammed. I assailed it with my pliers and a screw driver. I pried and jimmied and pushed. Suddenly, the shackle let go and the bomb gracefully dropped. We were now over the Adriatic and I had no desire to watch it go down.

* * *

About this time, I finally showed up for an appointment with the Group PR officer. He'd been writing me notes for several weeks and I'd been too preoccupied or too lazy to respond. He simply wanted me to come up to group headquarters and have my official picture taken. His last note read more like an order and I graciously complied. He quickly had his assistant snap my photograph. (See the front cover.) "Why," I asked, "Was this so urgent?" His answer stayed with me for a while. He said that several new crews had been shot down before they were able to have their pictures taken and he had been reprimanded by his superiors. Was this a great army or what?

* * *

When we weren't flying or training or whatever, we were variously assigned to routine duties. One of the commonest for squadron officers was censoring the mail. Every day, all the mail posted by the enlisted men of the squadron would be divided up among a few officers to be read and censored. It was mind numbing work. Rarely did anyone write anything that might have aided or abetted the enemy, but these men would scrawl the broadest assortment of platitudes that I could possibly have imagined. The shameful feeling of reading someone else's mail quickly faded and undiluted tedium took its place. After reading this fascinating stuff for a few hours and signing my name to the outside of scores of envelopes, I was almost ready for a combat mission.

Once again, I think of Yosarian. On censorship duty, he arbitrarily scissored out certain words and signed the envelopes, "Washington Irving," or sometimes, "Irving Washington." But since *Catch 22*, hadn't yet been written, I was neither clever, nor desperate, enough to match Heller's mischievousness. We officers were, of course, expected to censor our own mail. I was young and relatively disingenuous, so I carefully followed the rules.

* * *

In mid-October we flew our first mission to Vienna. At the briefing that morning, there was all the groaning that always came with that target. S-2 told us the flak would be HIA—heavy, intense and accurate. The weather guy gloomily predicted a lot of undercast. Our colonel gravely wished us good luck. We took off, assembled into our mighty armada, and crossed the Adriatic into Yugoslavia and then Austria.

The target area was everything that we'd been told to expect. In other words, it was frightful. These were the guns of Vienna and saying that the flak was thick was an understatement of vast dimensions. It almost seemed that we would have to fly through it on instruments and that even the autopilot might bail out. The Germans were sending up what was known as a box barrage. Because they knew precisely what our course was, and that it couldn't be changed, they'd lay an enormous blanket of flak ahead of us—at our altitude—confidant that we would have to fly directly through it.

I was toggling that day—salvoing my bombs when the squadron leader dropped his. This, sadly, gave me too much time to look around. I saw at least two B-24s from our group well hit. One caught fire and the other began a downward spiral. Although chutes were seen, I was not able to count them from my forward position. After bombs away, the pilot racked our airplane over to get us the hell out of there as quickly as possible. The sky was filled with dozens of airplanes doing the same thing and the flak was everywhere.

Suddenly, there was a thunderous explosion close by. I felt a blow to my chest. It was a piece of shrapnel the size of my fingertip. My flak suit had stopped it and I was home free. No Purple Heart this time. Later, I had the ugly little fragment of jagged steel set into a ring, which I promptly lost. I guess my name wasn't on that bit of German metal.

Some bad news on the intercom and I returned to the flight deck. Our engineer was lying on the floor and there was blood everywhere. His right foot had been almost blown off by a big piece of flak. The jagged hole it made in the fuselage must have been six inches across. One of our gunners had once been a medical technician and he was trying to stop the bleeding. There was little that the rest of us could do.

We were heading home and I was alive after my sixth and most terrible mission. And what about those two airplanes I saw go down—and the twenty guys who were flying them—not to mention the airplanes I didn't see go down? Why them and not us? What exquisite differences in the timing by the German gunners, the differences in the setting of their fuses, the differences in their calculations of wind and altitude and air speed that have spared us from a direct hit? Was God watching us and not them? What God? Whose God?

I once read something by a man in the British Bomber Command—a Halifax pilot—about these missions over enemy territory. "The line between the living and the dead was very thin. If you live on the brink of death yourself, it is as if those who have gone [down] have merely caught an earlier train to the same destination. And whatever that destination is, you will be sharing it soon, since you will almost certainly be catching the next train."

As we made our final approach, I fired red flares with the Very pistol. Wounded aboard. We landed and as always, I watched the runway flowing directly under us like a metal river. Suddenly we were crossing that river. We'd blown a tire, or rather the enemy flak had blown our tire, and we were veering crazily this way and that. The landing gear collapsed and we finally came to a stop. An ambulance noisily arrived and we helped to gently lift down the engineer. Then, as we have been trained to do, we abandoned that airplane within seconds.

The immediate problem was that the rest of the Group was also trying to land, the aircraft were bunched together as close as possible. Some of them had been damaged, some might also have had wounded aboard, and all of them were low on fuel. Our motionless airplane was squarely in the way and must be quickly jettisoned. Sure enough, even as we scrambled to get out, a heavy crane lumbered up and flipped our ship over on its back and off the runway. It would never fly again. The other guys could now land and Uncle Sam had just lost another very expensive airplane.

We were debriefed. What could we say? It was a bad trip—a real bad trip. There were still a couple of hours of daylight left so I sat on the slope of the hill overlooking the flight line to flush out the overwhelming feelings of the day and to write a not so epic poem. (It is reproduced in its original form at the end of this book.)

CHAPTER 17

Although we constantly wrestled with ambivalence—the intense fear of flying versus the no less forceful yearning to go home—these decisions were entirely out of our hands. The weather that winter was abominable. It was so cold that we would return from sub-zero missions to spend our ground time shivering in front of our impotent gasoline stoves. It also was so cloudy over most of Europe that we had far more sorties scrubbed than were ever flown. For example, during November, December, and January, I flew just four missions.

This led to a deadly sameness to our days—each day blending into the next with very little to mark it. On stand down days, we'd lie in our warm sacks until the last possible moment and then dash to breakfast just before the mess hall closed. Like most soldiers, we slept a lot. To shorten our days, we began to look forward to such dreary duties as Mess Officer and Officer of the Day. Even censor duty didn't seem all that bad. We scoured the neighborhood Red Cross clubs for reading matter. We attended the occasional training lecture with surprising equanimity.

Another occasional duty call was to be the officer-courier to pick up the Group mission orders for the next day. One night, with some trepidation, I set out with a jeep and driver, another vehicle ahead of us and one behind. All of us were armed, I with my trusty .45, the rest with carbines or other weapons. It was midnight. We drove to the 55th Wing Headquarters in Spinazzola—a dozen miles or so. I received and signed for the dispatch case with the next day's orders from Wing S-2 and we then headed home.

Now, with my secret orders tucked under my arm, my active imagination pictured a Nazi agent behind every tree. But we drove back uneventfully to our Group where I handed the dispatch case to the night duty guys. To my knowledge, nothing hostile had ever happened to a courier during the year that the 465th Group was in Italy, but that evening did supply me with a little extra gusto.

* * *

With all the time we had on our hands that winter, we played a lot of cards. There was a continuous bridge game in the Officers Club. One afternoon, after coming in from a mission—an easy one as it happened—the four of us, without missing a beat, played the same hand we had bid the night before. On the evenings after payday, came the serious poker games and some really belligerent crap games. The losers would lick their wounds and the winners would send home their money orders.

* * *

The social makeup of the 780th Squadron must have been similar to every other military unit in the Army. There were the same proportions of ethnic, religious, and geographic backgrounds found among all groups of young men in the 1940s. (Except, of course, there were no blacks.) Although religion and national origin were not talked about much, the actual regions that these guys came from were constantly being flaunted. One pilot, for example, had a daily mantra—"I'm from big D in beautiful T." Like all Texans, he believed that the sun never set on his blessed state. And then there was the Mississippi bombardier who seemed to have never left Mississippi.

Many of these men were from rural or small town America and were astonishingly unworldly. The few of us from big cities sometimes found conversation with these guys was complicated. Common ground was in short supply.

> How can you guys live in that crowded city?—like ants!
> Whatta you do if an elevator falls?
> Where do you park?
> Do you know your neighbor's name?
> Do you lock your doors every night?"

It was almost as if we lived on another planet. Nevertheless, there was also a built in camaraderie, partly because we were stuck here together for an indeterminate length of time, and partly because we were all engaging in a dangerous line of work.

One thing we flying personnel did have in common was our youth—most of us were still in our early twenties. This was an almost unique characteristic of the air services since top physical condition, rapid reaction time, and a high degree of eye and hand coordination were essential. The result of this selection process was an entire hierarchy of young folks.

Because of constant attrition—both from enemy action and from completion of our tours of duty—there was a continuing turnover of leadership. Thus, we had twenty-two year old pilots responsible for millions of dollars worth of airplanes and the lives of ten men in each. We also had twenty-seven year old lieutenant-colonels leading groups of several dozen of those airplanes, and we had thirty-five year old brigadier generals leading wings of several hundred. In other words, vast responsibilities lay on the shoulders of some very young men. And has that not always been true of war?

* * *

Our meals must be described as commonplace at best, and mediocre the rest of the time. When I was back in the States, we were always told that the good stuff was going overseas. Now that I was overseas and in an easily supplied area, hundreds of miles behind enemy lines, and enjoying (?) the status of a combat flier, the food should have been the best the Army had to offer. It wasn't. It was canned lima beans, a hundred and six varieties of Spam, and the ubiquitous shit-on-a-shingle.

* * *

We flew another heavy-intensive-accurate kind of mission, this time to the oil refineries of Blechhammer in Silesia. The guys called it "Black Hammer" and for good reasons. Once more a paralyzing gauntlet of fire. It was bad. But we got through it and headed home. An hour later, our number four engine began losing power and the pilot had to feather the prop. Although a B-24 is supposed to fly easily on three engines, for some reason we were losing altitude. I tried to work out an equation balancing the distance we were from Italy and our rate of descent. It was pretty serious arithmetic.

Our pilot decided we would have to bail out, even though we were over Yugoslavia and unsure of how friendly the natives were. He turned on the autopilot, I opened the bomb bay doors, and all nine of us squeezed ourselves onto the catwalk and looked down many thousands of feet. The airplane began rocking a bit and the pilot climbed back up to the cockpit to try and steady it. Several minutes went by and I went up to see what was going on. Our pilot, after glimpsing the Adriatic ahead, and surveying all his instruments, said he thought we could make it. So we all went back to our stations. We nicely cleared the Adriatic and limped back to our own little home. Maybe all's well that ends well, but it was pretty scary looking all that way down.

After debriefing, an S2 officer came up to tell me that my own crew—Steiner the pilot, Rondeau the co-pilot, Heymann the navigator and the six gunners that I had spent five months training with, had not returned. There were several reports that their airplane was hit after leaving the target and had dropped out of our formation. No one seemed to have any other information.

Wearily, I walked back to my tent. I collapsed on my cot. Soon, I roused myself and without even a sideward glance at the three empty cots, I headed for a depressing supper. My friends from other crews try to cheer me up. "They'll be back tomorrow," everyone said. Maybe they would, but somehow I couldn't seem to eat much, in spite of the fact that breakfast had been fifteen hours earlier.

I went back to my tent. What was I supposed to do now, I wondered? Do I pack up their stuff to be shipped home? Should I write a letter to their families? Rondeau had been married just the weekend before we went overseas. It occurred to me that even though we'd been living together all these months, I didn't know anyone's home address. I went to bed, but I couldn't sleep. Finally, the accumulated fatigue of this remarkable day knocked me out.

The crew did return to our squadron in a couple of days. Their airplane was hit several times over the target, lost an engine and suffered damage to another. The intercom had been shot out and Al Heymann, alone in the nose and believing the ship was going down, bailed out. He would be a German prisoner for the remainder of the war. The rest of the crew made a forced landing and spent two nights at an Allied airbase on the Yugoslav coast.

* * *

One of the interesting aspects of our downtime—the days we weren't flying—was the contrast between the physical hardship, the cold, and the terror of the six or eight hours of a mission and the total serenity of our squadron base. Well before I arrived at the 780th, there had been some bombing alerts, but now the area was as safe as any U.S. city. Unlike the guys in muddy trenches, our moments of danger, although painfully real, were limited to our "working hours." The rest of the time, we were reasonably comfortable and certainly secure. It made for a different kind of a war.

An even more dramatic separation between battles and home was found among the aircrews of the Eighth Air Force in England. Their bases were surrounded by livelier and more hospitable towns than we had in Southern Italy. They had pubs and friendly girls, and a familiar language, and there was always London. It must have made their frightening missions seem even more disconnected from their everyday lives.

* * *

As previously mentioned, getting around was seldom a problem. It was usually possible to reach Naples or Rome or other distant points by hitching a ride on an airplane, since old, tired B-24s were used to ferry guys to those cities or to rest camps on a regular basis. For close-in towns such as Bari or Foggia, there was a constant stream of jeeps and trucks going in every direction. But not unlike the illogical demands we make for transportation today, most guys still wanted their own wheels.

Early on, I had bought an old British motorcycle that, along with dozens of others, had been flown over from North Africa when the group first arrived in Italy. Fortunately, it was cheap because it lasted only a month or two before irrevocably blowing a cylinder. It did give me a sense of independence during its short life and I learned a bit about the rural neighborhoods around our field.

One dreary evening, Steiner and I were on our way home from Bari after doing some bars. We had hitched a ride as far as Canosa—about ten or twelve miles from the base—and were walking towards the crossroads to get another hitch when we passed the local Military Police station. There was a jeep sitting out in front with its engine running.

In Italy, jeeps were invariably kept as secure as possible. Locks and chains were often used, but a more common practice was to simply remove a vital part, such as the distributor head. Even this was not foolproof since there were GIs who carried extra distributors in their pocket just in case they might run across a jeep without one. The "borrowing" of jeeps was an almost acceptable practice—part of the cost of doing business in a war zone. I'm not sure what, if anything, the top brass ever did about it.

I don't think we even hesitated. We leaped in, drove off—not slowly—and headed for home. While it was still dark, we scrounged up a can of khaki paint and obliterated all the MP insignia, gave the vehicle a new number and a crude 780th Squadron logo and we now had our very own jeep.

Its swan song was equally dramatic, although rather ignoble. After several pleasant weeks of driving ourselves and our friends everywhere imaginable, it was announced by our Squadron Adjutant—a humorless fellow, indeed — that the Wing Air Inspector was due for a routine visit and that any unauthorized vehicles must be disposed of. To make a long story short, we drove our jeep down to the creek below the airstrip and rolled it into the water. It sank out of sight with a few bubbles and for all I know, may be there still.

* * *

By this time, our crew, along with many other replacement crews, had enough missions under our belt to have developed some really idiosyncratic habits. Some folks might have even called them superstitions. It was an obsessive faith in a bewildering assortment of omens, talisman, and repetitive routines that seem to affect most combat crews. There were guys who carried rabbits feet, lucky coins, or trinkets from girlfriends. Others made a practice of doing some small thing—getting out of bed, putting on their clothes in the same order, climbing into the airplane, even combing their hair—exactly the same way before every mission. There were men who always wore the same shirt or socks that they'd worn on their first mission.

In short, if it was some bauble, some bit of clothing, some act, that we thought had kept us safe on an early mission, we simply wanted to keep carrying it, wearing it, or doing it the same way. This might be superstition, but we were still alive, so it must be working. In my case, I will confess, I never flew without my lucky scarf. I still have it, in my bottom drawer next to my old argyle socks.

CHAPTER 18

I was on still another awful mission—the aircraft factory at Wiener Neustadt, near Vienna. We'd been there before, but the Germans had always rebuilt it. So we followed our customary track. Northeast over the Adriatic, across the sanitized sections of Yugoslavia, and then due north to the target. Today, I was with a relatively new crew and I was the navigator. I would toggle out my bombs when I saw the squadron leader release his.

I sat at my little desk, bundled up in my bulky wardrobe and connected to the usual life support systems. The weather was good and there was only a scattered undercast—most of the world below was visible. Hence, I was using pilotage, although I also had to keep my dead reckoning log in case the weather changed. If we were not heading towards a possible Armageddon, I might have actually enjoyed this trip. The sea was very blue, the Dalmatian coast was dramatic and far to our east I could just make out beautiful Lake Balaton. I was not really in the mood for scenic charm, but all of this is useful when doing pilotage.

We arrived at our IP and swung towards the target. The lead bombardiers were doing their maddenly slow work and

I could only look out from my Plexiglas viewing perch at the terrible deluge of black flak bursts. We salvoed our bombs just as a shell exploded close by. We were hit. Number four engine was history and the pilots immediately feathered the prop. We left the target area in a steep diving turn. I called for a damage report and no one was hurt, but there were a lot of holes all over the airplane. With only three engines, we were losing altitude and falling behind our group. The pilot asked for a heading home and I quickly reckoned it, hoping that we would see no enemy fighters. A straggler, which is what we now were, could be an easy mark for the Luftwaffe.

Our other operating systems—hydraulics, oxygen, intercom, gas lines—all seemed okay and we gratefully noted that two Little Friends, P-51 Mustangs, were watching over us. The number one engine started to sound ragged. Sure enough, it soon gave up its internal combustion ghost and we were now really limping along on two engines. There was little chance we could even reach the Adriatic, not to mention cross it. We were rapidly losing altitude and I looked through all my maps for a friendly airstrip where we could put this bird down. We were over Russian-held Hungary and I had a chart of possible emergency airfields. I found one fairly close—somewhere in northwestern Hungary—and I gave the pilot the heading.

We were at just a few thousand feet when we spotted it, a single grass strip with a couple of small buildings at one end. The strip seemed barely long enough, but we airborne beggars couldn't be choosers. There was no radio presence here, and in any case we didn't have any frequency numbers. We skipped the base and downwind legs and made a final approach, hoping there wasn't much wind. As we got closer we saw tracer bullets coming at us from several gun emplacements. They were not very accurate and there was nothing we could do about them anyway. We made a bumpy, but acceptable landing—probably our pilot's first one on grass—and turned around and taxied towards the buildings. Their guns were now silent. I followed my instructions vis-a-vis the Bombardier's Oath, aimed my .45 at the eyepiece of the bombsight and destroyed it. I felt like Willie in the famous Mauldin cartoon, shooting his faithful jeep after it broke down.

We climbed out of our wounded airplane and warily watched the men strolling towards us. I had my hand on my .45 although God knows what I would have done with it at this point. They were clearly Soviet soldiers and their leader, we figured out later, was a major. We all pointed to the American flag patches on our jackets and they started to shout "Americanski" and we knew we were okay. They seemed very glad to see us. The reason they fired they tell us, at least I think it was what they said, was that the Germans had strafed them a few weeks earlier in a captured B-24. Their small detachment had been on this field for some time and they had plainly been dying of boredom. We might have been their first visitors since they got here.

The major was all gold toothed smiles, but not much English beyond Americanski and tovarisch. There was a young lieutenant, however, who had a workable, if heavily accented, command of Soviet taught English. We were invited into the larger of two cement buildings. It was a headquarters office, eating place, kitchen, and day room.

First things first, so we were all offered cups of vodka and we politely accepted. It was beginning to get dark so they lighted some oil lamps—no electricity here. It was supper time and we were offered some pretty good soup and rather old bread. We talked, and the lieutenant, translating for the major, told us that they could drive us to a railhead the next day in one of their trucks. From there we could get a train to Budapest and maybe find someone to fly us back to Italy.

We discussed this for a while and everything seemed fine. Then the major asked us what we wanted to do about our airplane. We knew, of course, that it would never fly again. The latest model B-24s were now streaming into Italy, the Army was not about to send mechanics and new engines to this remote field to fix up an old wreck, and at worst, the war would be over in a few months. So our pilot sort of shrugged.

"Can we have it?" the major asked. Our guy shrugged again. "We'll buy it." the lieutenant translated. We all looked at each other. Why not, it wasn't going anywhere, we silently agreed. We asked how much they wanted to offer. Since we were all bushed and to make a long story a bit shorter, we settled on a few bottles of vodka and some Soviet cigarettes. Our co-pilot was inspired to write up a bill of sale and I tore off a piece of my navigator log. We three officers duly signed it and now everything was legal. I wondered only momentarily what U.S. laws we'd broken and whether anybody would ever find out. I decided that no one would even care.

We also traded a few of our Colt.45s for some Soviet and German pistols. When our co-pilot handed over his .45, the major pointed it straight up and fired. I looked up and saw that the ceiling was pockmarked with dozens of holes and figured that shooting upward must be some kind of Russian sport.

We tried to make ourselves comfortable on the concrete floor. We had our flying clothes for warmth and parachute packs for pillows and it wasn't too bad. But some time after midnight we were awakened by gunfire. It was dark and very cold. Someone said that the Russians were shooting off the machine guns on our airplane and shouldn't we do something? Someone else said that the airplane now belonged to them. Didn't they pay for it? We went back to sleep.

The next morning we all climbed onto a GMAC lend-lease truck and, accompanied by our English-speaking lieutenant, we set out. Two hours later, we were crammed into a compartment on a train chugging through the

Hungarian countryside. We arrived in Budapest quite late, the lieutenant rustled up some kind of dried fish and stale bread, and we bunked down on the floor of a railroad office. Another truck appeared in the morning—this time a Dodge—and our guide took us on a speedy sightseeing tour of Pest, which is the industrial part of the city and was pretty bombed out. We couldn't get across the Danube to the more historic and beautiful Buda because so many bridges had been destroyed.

We ended up at a Soviet controlled airfield and waited in a damaged hanger. Three other Americans joined us. Two of them were the only survivors of their B-24 crew on the same Wiener Neustadt raid we'd been on. The other guy was a P-51 fighter pilot who also had had some bad luck. After a long wait, we were led a few hundred yards to where a lend-lease American C-47 was parked and we were all invited to clamber aboard. There were no seats or parachutes.

The Soviet pilots arrived and the engines were started. We were parked almost on the runway and we took off at once under full throttle. There was no preflight, no warm up of the engines, no attempt to check instruments, no testing of the magnetos, nothing. We were all a little nervous, but except for some ineffective small arms fire over Croatia, the flight back to Italy was uneventful. We landed near Foggia and the C-47 immediately took off again. Our squadron exec sent a truck for us and we arrived back at 780th in time for dinner. We had been away less than 60 hours—two nights—but no one seemed to have missed us.

* * *

It was time, we were told, to enjoy a leave at an Army rest camp—the Isle of Capri. "Rest, Recreation and Rehabilitation" (RRR) it was called. The fabled isle was restful enough—although it was too cold to be very recreative and

I don't remember much rehabilitation. We were billeted in the majestic Quisisana Hotel. The food was great, the white tablecloths, gleaming silver, and impeccable service were splendid. There were real mattresses and sheets and maids and best of all was the awesome bathroom (with the first bidet I'd ever seen and into which I innocently peed).

Along with the hundreds of AAF officers was a small cadre of nurses and WAAC officers, plus a few local signorinas. One evening a dance was held and I dressed in my Class A uniform proudly garnished with whatever ribbons I had earned. It was not until I joined the festivities—noting that there was just one girl for each dozen men—that I understood that Second Lieutenants were on the same level as the Italian waiters. Everywhere I looked, I saw majors and colonels and even two generals. It was a chastening experience.

I read a lot. I hiked around the small island. I stood on Tiberius's Leap where, according to legend, the exalted emperor cast his victims into the sea, and I contemplated that vast sea. I thought of the rulers who had visited this tiny island—the sovereign, the omnipotent, the bloodthirsty. There were the Caesars and the Saracens, Barbarossa and Napoleon, and let's not forget Il Duce. What an awful procession.

When the week was over, although I may have been rested, I was curiously restless. I wasn't especially eager to get shot at again, but I did want to get on with things and finish my tour of duty. Capri was okay—Chicago would be better.

* * *

The Commanding Officer (CO) of the 780th was a Lieutenant Colonel, a reclusive man whom I seldom saw, and spoke with even less. He had headed the squadron since it was first activated back in Nebraska, and I had heard grumblings that some guys no longer wanted to fly with him.

Be that as it may, I was quite distant from all that. One day, however, as we lounged on the flight line, waiting for the green takeoff flare, the colonel drove up and announced that he was going to fly with us as an observer. Our co-pilot was dismissed, the colonel climbed into the righthand seat and we took off.

It was a unexceptional mission to Bologna, with only light resistance. But somehow, we suffered several large flak holes in the waist area and although there was no damage to any of our vital parts, it had scared hell out of the gunners back there. As we began our homeward journey, the colonel squeezed through the bomb bays into the waist of the airplane. I was already there checking the damage. The holes seemed enormous and the two gunners, now sitting on the deck, were not surprisingly, looking very pale. As it happened, one of them, a young sergeant, had obviously not been to the squadron barber for a while and had grown rather bushy sideburns.

The colonel, with scarcely a glance at the flak holes, and not a comforting word about the gunners' providential escape, fastened his gaze on the hairy gunner. He told him he was a sorry example of a non-commissioned officer and that he, the colonel, would see about removing some of his, the sergeant's, stripes. He then turned and squeezed his way forward to the flight deck. I found myself speechless and the sergeant looked like he was ready to bail out on the spot. It was a classic example of military authoritarianism, and how chicken shit the army can be even under combat conditions.

* * *

Some weeks later, Rondeau, our co-pilot, and I caught another B-24 ride to Naples. We looked up a family that someone had recommended to us, presented them with some fresh and very precious eggs that we had bartered for back at camp, and moved into their extra room for the weekend. It was a tidy small apartment in a scabrous part of town, but it suited us and we visited them several times. There were three grade school children in the family and we enjoyed a couple of hilarious evenings trying to build a cultural exchange.

Naples, of course, gave us access to the ruins of Pompeii, which seemed the very apex of tourism. Especially noteworthy was one of the Pompeii houses with carvings and frescos that were so lurid to my unsophisticated Midwestern eyes that I could hardly suppress my astonishment. Our guide barred the way for several American nurses who were in our party. Times have certainly changed.

* * *

About this time, we participated in what was called a "maximum effort." It was a mission to a target at the very farthest point of our operating range. I seem to remember it was Brux, Germany, but since we did not actually get there because of weather, I have no record of it. We had flown on other so-called maximum effort missions, but this one included most of the Eighth Air Force out of England as well as our Fifteenth out of Italy. It added up to several thousand bombers and hundreds of fighters and although we could see only a small part of it, it was truly massive. I later read that from the ground, the formations of airplanes took hours to pass and the sky was black with them.

I cannot even guess as to the effect this fearful performance must have had on the German people.

* * *

Behold! It was suddenly Christmas, but in light of every Christmas past, it was a gloomy affair. A few paper-decorated stunted trees and some half-hearted caroling was the extent of it. Even our packages from home arrived long after.

The weather steadily worsened. Sometimes, missions would be cancelled before we even awakened. Sometimes we would troop down to the flight line, prepare the airplane, and suit up only to see the red flares indicating another scrubbed mission. And often, we would take off, assemble our immense formations, head for the target, face total cloud cover, and finally turn back to Italy—a waste of several cold hours.

About this time some new technology that could actually deal with this cloud cover, made a belated appearance. We called it "Mickey" and a specially trained guy operated it. It was a radar scope, quite crude by today's standards, that could "see" the target through the undercast. It meant that eventually, fewer missions would be cancelled because of weather.

* * *

It was late winter—and one would have thought that by now I would be reasonably fluent in Italian. I wish I could report that I had taken advantage of those wasted days on the ground by doing something useful. There was surely an abundance of native Italians around. Whether because we Americans were so intent on talking only to each other, or because of weather imposed sloth, language study was not a priority. We did, however, routinely adopt certain Italian words, and it was interesting how those few could convey our not-so-elevated thoughts. The result was a sub-standard pidgin Italian. For example, these two airman are having a drink together:

> Rough mission, eh paesano,
> Si, it was no fucking buono.
> Anybody morto?
> Possibile.
> Similare Vienna eh? Multi flak?
> Si.

CHAPTER 19

Although our weather into the early spring was mostly bad, now and then we would savor a few nice days. There was some splendid scenery as we flew over southern Europe. We saw Naples, Rome, and Bologna; we saw Venice and Florence on several lovely days; we flew to, or near, Munich, Salzburg, and of course, Vienna; we flew alongside the forbidding and snow covered Alps many times.

And as we approached those major cities, sometimes to merely pass by, and sometimes to drop our bombs, I would often think about Chicago, or New York, or San Francisco. Big cities greatly resemble each other from 25,000 feet. Was it too much of a stretch to imagine flying over my Chicago hometown with 500 pound bombs?

One very bright day we headed to Muldorf, a medium-sized town near Munich. There was, inexplicably, only light flak on the long bomb run. The town lay ahead of us, peaceful and quiet, and our view was picture perfect. We were in the second group and as I watched this tranquil Bavarian landscape through my bombsight, it suddenly exploded in a storm of flame, smoke and rising wreckage.

The bombs of the leading squadrons had squarely found their mark, and it was, indeed, a clear and dreadful image.

* * *

I have often thought about the word remorse, and when I returned home after the war, I would occasionally be asked if I ever felt any. I suppose I did, but a more honest answer would have been that most of the time I was (a) too busy doing what I was supposed to be doing; (b) too unnerved to think about anyone but myself; (c) too intent on rationalizing that those folks down there were Nazis and look what they had been doing to Europe in general and to the Jews in particular. This last cop-out was okay when applied to the guilty, but didn't help much when I thought about the innocent. I wondered if Genghis Khan or the Grand Inquisitor or Heinrich Himmler had ever worried about such niceties. For that matter, do the folks responsible for air pollution or clear cutting or urban sprawl ever feel remorse? Can they buy redemption?

But if my sense of contrition was underdeveloped in those days, has it changed through the many years that have separated me—insulated me—from that unhappy time? Certainly, when I think about it, I feel remorseful. It is, however, a perception of sorrow rather than one of guilt.

Which, of course, brings up the whole complex question of the accountability of soldiers. From the Nuremberg Nazi elite to the lowly German privates who helped guard Treblinka, the cry was that they were simply following orders. Why can't it be argued that I was also simply following orders? As a matter of fact, the penalty for refusing to follow an order was undoubtedly far more severe for a Wehrmacht soldier than for an American flyer. The former was likely to be shot; the latter merely demoted and put on garbage detail.

Historical revisionism has become fashionable these days.

Simply ignoring the fact that Allied air power shortened the war and saved thousands of lives on both sides, revisionists delight in pointing out what they happen to consider were the strategic bombing lapses during WW II. It's too easy to say that the air assaults of Berlin, Dresden, Tokyo, and of course, Hiroshima and Nagasaki were wicked. Unfortunately, there was a war going on—the greatest and deadliest in world history—and ordinary men had to make extraordinary decisions.

In spite of any feelings of remorse—and they were few—and in spite of some serious fear, we all kept flying. I don't think anyone was doing it to protect the flag. Some guys—John Hersey called them "War Lovers"—flew because they liked it; some, because it was a job that had to be done; some, because they didn't want to let their fellow fliers down; and the rest of us because quitting was even worse than continuing. The stigma of refusing the next mission, while ill-defined, was something to be avoided at all cost. There were a few men who managed to withdraw from combat—actually leave the squadron. These guys were quietly hustled off the base and most of us felt uneasy about it. So it came down to peer pressure—not wanting other guys to think you were chicken. Remorse was a distant second.

Fear was more palpable. Peer pressure did nothing to sublimate fear. I remember a pilot named Frank who collected a half-dozen armored flak suits and carefully distributed them around his pilot seat. Most of us thought that was excessive and he became known as Fearless Frank. Fear was always with us and if we forgot about it momentarily, it lurched back quickly. Fear has been described as a pervasive dark presence, as a malaise so physical that it could make one throw up, or even crap in one's pants. My own fear was formless and ubiquitous. It was simply there. Somehow, in some way, most of us developed an understanding of fear—perhaps not mastery, but at least an accommodation.

The relatively pleasant recess that came as we left a

terrible target and were homeward bound, or the busy card games that diverted us when we had reached home base, were only short respites. Then we would have to pass Go and move on to the Operations Tent blackboard to read the menacing battle orders for tomorrow.

It was dangerous up in those German skies, guys were getting killed, and I could only hope that I wouldn't be one of them.

I could hope, but could I pray? Prayer was a subject that was seldom discussed. There must have been many men in the squadron who earnestly practiced their religious faith, and others who were only relatively pious. I was too preoccupied to know. I don't even remember if there was any sort of church on the field.

On my early missions, I tried some prayer. I had once learned the 23rd Psalm and I would recite it, woefully emphasizing the "walk through the valley of the shadow of death." But although I did fear evil, I was not especially comforted by His rod and His staff. The real dilemma was my feeling of hypocrisy. Could I recite that Psalm; could I even pretend to pray, just because I was suddenly facing great danger? If my background included little faith, if I had never been even slightly worshipful in my previous life, how could I talk to God *In extremis?*

So I discontinued my prayers and continued my fear.

* * *

I sometimes think about the guys I knew, and naturally, the thousands of guys I didn't know, who are buried in those American cemeteries in Italy. I contemplate the nearly sixty years of life I've had since those awful days—the fine things I've done; the pleasures I've enjoyed; the sounds of my children and my grandchildren; the love of my wife. All of this denied to those men who died in the skies of Europe.

We are wasteful, we survivors, and we too infrequently

count up our blessings, recognize our good fortune, or greet each new day as one more benefaction.

I have visited a number of WW II cemeteries and as I look out at the countless crosses and stars of David, I am filled with sadness and a sense of wonder. Might one of those men, I ask myself, have discovered a cure for cancer or an antidote for AIDS? Could there be a guy buried there who might have helped devise a new plan for world peace? Might one of those men have worked out a recipe for our faltering schools?

No one responds. The white crosses and stars simply stare back at me.

CHAPTER 20

Because our crew had accumulated enough missions, or maybe because we just looked tired, we were allowed another RRR week, this time in Rome. We flew there, found beds in a temporary bachelor officer quarters (BOQ) and Rondeau and I hurried out to see the town. We "did" Rome just as millions of other tourists have before and since. The Forum, the Pantheon, the Piazza Navona, Via Veneto, and on and on.

It was still too cold for outdoor cafes so our carousing was confined to an American joint called the Arizona Club. Rome was filled with soldiers, mostly American, and of course, the Romans themselves—shadowy, tattered and frayed. The city was certainly not the *bella Roma* my wife and I have enjoyed over so many postwar years.

One morning, a navigator named Maguire, from the 464th, asked if I wanted to go with him to the Vatican. The Pope held an audience every day for Allied servicemen, and my friend, a practicing Catholic, figured he might be able to earn some divine influence. I thought that maybe it wouldn't hurt me to have a little extra leverage on my next mission—or maybe just another shot of hypocrisy.

On our way to St. Peters, we passed a guy selling small metal crosses. We each bought one. We took our places with several dozen other guys in uniform and after some papal preliminaries, Pope Pius XII came down the aisle. Maguire held out his cross to be blessed and so did I. There was a brief ceremony in Latin and it was over.

Maguire said he would carry his cross on his next mission. I decided to simply keep mine as a souvenir. Some years later on a date, I gave it to a Catholic girl who was naturally impressed. Contrary to what some of my friends suggested, she did not come across for that cross.

* * *

Back to work. Winter was easing itself out, the war was slowly coming to a close, but the German cannon were even more concentrated and our missions were surely no less perilous. Also, about this time the Luftwaffe sprang a late surprise. The ME 163 and its twin-engine version, the ME 262, were the first jet-powered military aircraft in history. I later heard that an American jet fighter was scheduled to appear in October of 1945, but the war was over by then, and that airplane was delayed even longer by a number of problems.

I saw the German jet only once. It flew through our formation at a speed we simply couldn't believe. For some reason, it did not shoot at us, and we couldn't shoot at it. We were so astonished that we wouldn't have been able to hit it anyway. We were told the jet flew a hundred mph faster than our P-51s. Fortunately, the Germans weren't able to build very many of these incredible airplanes, and in any case, it was much too late in the war. But the might-have-beens were scary.

On April 12, we flew to northern Italy to bomb a railroad bridge and as we headed home we got the stunning news on Armed Forces Radio that President Roosevelt had died in Georgia. I was nearly five miles above enemy territory when I learned that my commander-in-chief was dead.

It was a transcendent sort of moment. Franklin Delano Roosevelt had been president all of my adult life and the sudden reality of his death was almost too much to bear. I was ten when he was elected; fifteen the day I saw him dedicate a new Chicago bridge and give his famous speech demanding that aggressive nations be quarantined; eighteen when he was elected to an unprecedented third term. He had become president during the Great Depression and he died just before our final dazzling victories in WW II. I wept into my oxygen mask.

* * *

As the war ran down, the number of rumors of what was going to happen to us ratcheted up. Many were quite fanciful—we would go home; we would go to Japan; we would go home and then go to Japan. A point system had been announced, with points for months of service and months overseas, and extra points for certain combat experience. Few of us had enough points at that moment, but we could still begin counting. Also, at this time, our long awaited promotions began to trickle in. I turned in my gold bar for the silver of a first louie, and Steiner became a captain, with only a touch of arrogance.

Not unexpectedly, interest in Japan began to quicken. I was appointed an Information and Education Officer and delegated to instruct everyone in the squadron on the geography, history, and culture of the Land of the Rising Sun. With this assignment, came a whole library of Army booklets on those subjects so I spent several evenings skimming them and soon was more or less an expert. Over the next few weeks, I held a dozen seminars and in spite of some personal misgivings concerning my grasp of Japanese geopolitics, along with a noticeable lack of enthusiasm on the part of my audience, I felt I had contributed something to the Pacific war effort.

* * *

Our last mission—my thirty-first—was on April 25th to Linz, Austria. It was fearful—the Germans seemed to have dragged in every gun in Europe—and the mission was, in retrospect, totally unnecessary, a tragic example of bureaucratic overkill. VE Day would come only two weeks later.

A lot of airplanes were hit that day and the Germans, we were told, were taking no prisoners. Our squadron lost only one plane, but the group lost more. The flak was inescapable. As we approached the target during the usual interminable bomb run, our nose-gunner shouted over the intercom,

"Holy shit! I thought the war was almost over."
"The Germans haven't been told yet," someone said.
"Just drop the fucking bombs," the pilot said.
"Bombs away." I said.

* * *

So now there were no more missions and rumor-laden or not, we had to find things to do. The weather warmed quickly and baseball became the business of choice. There was all kinds of action, both softball and hardball. I was drafted as a home plate umpire, made a few really bad calls, but lived to apologize. On especially warm days, we piled into trucks, went off to the beaches of Barletta and dunked our pale white bodies in the Adriatic. Craps, poker, and bridge continued at a feverish pace. There was a full dress military formation, a ritual we had almost forgotten, to receive a Group Presidential Citation—our second—for valorous conduct. Many of us received individual decorations—mostly Air Medal clusters. Mine have been in my dresser drawer ever since, but might one day impress some of my grandchildren.

VE Day came on May 8th and with it a more solemn military ceremony with prayers for the men from our squadron who would not be going home. Then came the mother of all celebrations—free booze all day and a lot of handshaking and loud huzzahs. I wondered if after surviving all the *sturm und drang* of combat, I would finally succumb to cirrhosis of the liver—without even a Purple Heart.

What were my real feelings on this signal day—the day I'd been thinking about for such a long time? Relief, I suppose. Gratitude that I was still alive. I doubt if I was pondering the brave new postwar world, and a modern postwar kitchen with a shiny postwar dishwasher. I wasn't looking for apple pie and the pinafore-clad girl who might be waiting for me I was, however, worried about my chances of being pulled into the war in the Pacific.

* * *

Group ground personnel began to dismantle the entire station, which had grown into a bustling town of several thousand men, and to prepare for the long trip to the states. The huts, mess halls, medical buildings, clubs, and operation centers, would be left intact. We later heard that all of this unattractive architecture quickly became a new Italian village. A lot of heavy equipment was also left. The "ground pounders," as we called the non-flying folks, would eventually spend the summer traveling home by ship and transport plane.

We war-weary flying folks were expected to simply cross the Atlantic in our war-weary aircraft. This not only solved the problem of bringing us home, but also repatriated the airplanes. No one realized at the time that those faithful B-24s would soon be turned to scrap anyway.

As it happened, our crew's assigned airplane was the

legendary V-Grand, the 5000th B-24 Liberator built at the Consolidated-Vultee factory in San Diego. On her outer skin were scrawled the signatures, and sometimes the sentiments, of the thousands of factory workers who had helped build her. Steiner and the rest of our crew had not exactly volunteered for the honor of flying her home. V-Grand had had a troubled history and although she'd always returned from her missions, her record of recurrent bruises was intimidating.

CHAPTER 21

Before I actually started home, I was presented with a tempting proposal. A pilot and co-pilot from another crew I'd flown with several times, and who were good friends of mine, had decided to explore post-war Europe and had invited me to come along. They'd asked our CO for a jeep—there were dozens sitting around—and more important, they'd asked for open orders that would enable them to move anywhere at will. How they finagled this, I'll never know, but those undated orders allowed them to eat, sleep, and even draw partial pay from any of the hundreds of U.S. Army installations in Europe. I thought about it, but finally said no, and within a few days, they were gone.

Long after the war, I spoke by phone several times to one of them. They had spent the summer driving several thousand miles through war-ravaged Europe. They had seen many of the cities we had bombed—the description of the damage to our *bete noir*, Vienna, was of particular interest. They had seen concentration camps, refugees by the thousands, and as few others had, they saw the consequences of WW II in its appalling entirety. I look back at my refusal to join those guys that summer as one of the dumbest things I have ever done. I simply wanted to go home.

* * *

Late in May, we packed up our personal stuff—surprisingly sparse considering that we'd been in Italy for so long—and flew to a field near Taranto, a large town on the instep of Italy's boot. This had been an Italian air force base and the living conditions were Spartan. It was, for example, my first encounter with the infamous Turkish style standup toilets which clearly take some getting used to.

At last, we left *bella Italia* and crossed the Mediterranean on an eight hour flight to Morocco and the exotic (at least to us) city of Marrakech. In the few days we had there, we managed to tour most of the city and spend some hours exploring the souks of the endlessly fascinating Medina. We were a handful of westerners wandering in a sea of North Africans. There were no tourists, of course, and I somehow felt like a nineteenth century adventurer—perhaps a French colonist, or more likely, Peter Lorre as Pepe LaMoko in the Casbah.

Another long hop to the Portuguese Azores and a couple of nothing days on an AAF field waiting for the weather to clear to the west.

* * *

We finally took off for what turned out to be a ten-hour hair-raising transatlantic trip. For one thing, we had a brand new navigator—he'd flown only one mission—and in the middle of the North Atlantic, he became quite lost.

Since dead reckoning while flying over the ocean is exceedingly inaccurate and pilotage is naturally impossible, and since we were out of radio compass range, the only remaining option was celestial navigation. I had never been trained in those singular mysteries and it appeared that our navigator was not exactly a master. Furthermore, the skies were mostly obscured by high clouds. So we resolutely continued on our original heading and hoped that our low tech magnetic compass would be unerring.

Most of the crew, including me, slept most of the way. There was, after all, little else to do except worry, and whatever was going to happen was out of our hands. When we reached the point in time when we were supposed to be over Newfoundland there was a total undercast—nothing but nothingness below—and it was at this point that we discovered that our radio compass was not working. Steiner decided to let down to where there might be some visibility. We were all becoming just a little edgy because the fuel gauges were showing almost empty. As we quickly lost altitude, Steiner made another discovery. Our airspeed indicator was also not working, which meant that it would be very easy to stall this airplane and spin into the ground. No one was sleeping anymore.

We finally broke through the undercast at a few hundred feet, saw lots of barren land, but nothing in the way of a landmark. Now our gas was really getting low and I began to feel I was in a bad movie. After thirty-one paralyzing missions and countless attacks from German guns, were we to finally cash in our chips on some empty Canadian real estate? Still no radio compass, but our VHF radio was working and we could talk to and hear the control tower at Harmon Field. We didn't know where it was, but the guys there sounded friendly. We zigzagged around the increasingly bleak landscape.

Suddenly, we saw the field and directly made our final approach with no other nonsense. We landed and began to taxi to the operations building. First, our number four engine quit and a few minutes later, our number two. We limped along the taxiway on the remaining two engines and maybe a half-pint of gas. What a thrill.

We refueled, our airspeed indicator was repaired, but we, the crew, were not totally reassured. Still eager to get home, we took off once more for our last leg. Five hours later, on the Eighth of June, 1945, we landed at Bradley Field, Connecticut, U.S.A. We were thirty flying hours out of Italy. We climbed out, unloaded our gear and several of us unself-consciously kissed the tarmac. As we boarded the truck to take us to debriefing, I cast one last look at V-Grand, the big-assed bird that had brought us home. It turned out to be the last time I would see a B-24 until an airshow some fifty years later.

Almost, but not quite, home. Along with other crews heading west, we boarded a train, and as always, our destination was a murky secret. We decided that the army was really concerned about the Japanese finding out that we were going home.

CHAPTER 22

I had a forty-five day leave and with a couple of phone calls, I managed to parlay it into sixty. It seemed a vast amount of time, but it went by like the wind. I was one of the first of the returning veterans in that early summer of 1945 and I had a marvelous time.

* * *

But too soon it was over and following my orders, I took another train to a replacement depot in North Carolina. This was not a quiet rest camp. There were thousands of air crew people here, all combat veterans, all waiting for reassignment orders and all yearning to not go near Japan. I bumped into my pilot Steiner and we hung out at the officers club for couple of days, drinking and speculating.

I took the usual battery of tests—physical, mental and psychological—and desperately tried to flunk something. No such luck. My next orders were not long in coming. I was to report to Midland Army Air Field in Texas as an instructor at a bombardier training school. While this was better than operational training for the Pacific, West Texas was not high on my list of livable neighborhoods.

By train and a sweltering Greyhound I finally got there. The air field was between Odessa and Midland and ten zillion oil wells. Odessa had the blue-collar workers and the best bars. Midland had the millionaires—supposedly the most per capita in the U.S.—and a "luxury" hotel. The general area was sometimes called, and perhaps not unfairly, the asshole of America.

In any case, we were given no orders, no duties, no anything. We simply sat in a superheated officers club and played gin rummy day after day for a couple of weeks. Some nights we hitched into Midland, but that was also a downer. A bunch of old guys in big hats sitting around the ungrand hotel lobby and not talking—just looking. We also caught up with our back flight pay by taking a series of so-called training flights over empty Texas acreage. Once we landed in El Paso and spent an afternoon at a third rate bullfight across the border in Ciudad Juarez.

An Army Air Force B-29 dropped an atom bomb—we hadn't the foggiest idea what that was—but the radio commentators seemed to think it meant that the war was nearly over. Although few details on the bomb filtered in, I tried to understand the magnitude of the mission of the Enola Gay. As an experienced bombardier, I was just as bewildered as any civilian about what had happened at Hiroshima. I knew how big a crater my 500 pound bombs could dig, but an entire city? It was unimaginable. Many years would pass before I visited Hiroshima myself and saw the real dimensions of that bomb drop.

The war with Japan ended in mid August and unlike V-E Day, we had no wild celebration. It was simply too hot and too much of an anti-climax. In early September, I found a clerk who would listen and I cashed in my points for discharge. But before I could leave the office, the colonel in charge asked if I wouldn't like to sign up for the Army Air Force Reserve and be promoted to captain. Without missing a beat, I politely thanked him and said I wouldn't, and was handed my new orders to report to Fort Sheridan, Illinois. If I had opted for the Reserve, I probably would have been called back to active duty during the Korean war.

There was no sure way to get back to Chicago except the god-awful bus I had ridden earlier, so I hitchhiked—by truck, jeep, and an Army plane, and I made it. Back home, sort of, I found myself in a BOQ at Fort Sheridan, a long way from my parents' north-side apartment in Chicago and again with no duties but to wait for that elusive discharge. I had borrowed my father's prewar Studebaker so I was temporarily mobile.

* * *

The fall college term was already well underway, and I thought I should try to enroll somewhere and not waste another semester. I got a pass from Fort Sheridan, and found myself driving up to Lake Forest College and knocking on a door one rainy afternoon. The Director of Admissions was delighted to see me. He glanced at my transcript, offered me a degree in just three more semesters, and told me I was only the eighth veteran to enroll since the war had ended. He also announced that we eight, plus a dozen or so non-veteran men were faced with co-existing with seven-hundred women students. This unexpected reward for my unselfish assistance in winning the war, convinced me that I should enroll forthwith at LFC.

I signed everything in sight and the Director guided me to my new dorm room on the fifth floor of College Hall. What's more, he actually helped carry my bags up the five flights, a courtesy I'm sure few directors of admissions have ever offered. Lake Forest College certainly hungered for more male students.

Over the next several weeks I alternated my residence between College Hall and the BOQ at Fort Sheridan. I was still in uniform and that was not all bad. I fit quite comfortably into the macho image of the heroic flyer wearing my shabby thirty-one mission leather flight jacket. It helped to establish my personna on campus and surely bolstered my tender ego. I began enjoying the inexhaustible supply of young women that graced the LFC campus. It was a splendid semester, but at the beginning of the next term, my pleasant monopoly ended. Nearly a thousand male veterans shouldered their way into the school.

I was surprised to learn that the new GI Bill of Rights would cover a sizeable part of my undergraduate tuition and allow me to go on to the University of Chicago for an MBA. Although I gave it little thought at the time, it soon became apparent that the GI Bill would surely rank among the most important Congressional Acts in my lifetime. It enabled several million veterans to earn college degrees. Many of us would never have aspired to, nor could we have afforded a college education. And of course, it was this generation that would go on to build America into the greatest economic engine in world history.

My formal discharge came through at last, and after donning some odds and ends of civilian finery, I once again looked the part of a college boy. My first day as a private citizen came almost exactly three years after I had enlisted in Uncle Sam's Army Air Force. I had been rigorously trained in skills I would never use again; I had learned to get along with hundreds of men with backgrounds totally different than mine; I had been frightened beyond anything I could have ever envisaged; I had given up a meaningful piece of my adult life. Nonetheless, I was alive, twenty-three, and the whole world lay ahead.

* * *

When I reflect on this three year interruption of what could have been a routine university milestone, I am of several minds. It was an impermanent, but defining chapter of my early life. Although I was glad enough to have had the seasoning, I surely would not want to do it again. There is, of course, something to be said for military experience and its accompanying qualities of discipline and camaraderie. I also believe that wartime can add certain virtues to a country's social essence.

Why have I waited fifty years to reminisce about my small part in WW II? The truth is I don't know. There was college to finish, a business path to begin, a wife to cherish, and four kids to raise. I was not burdened with post combat stress. I suffered no nightmares nor other kinds of anxiety. I did not deliberately banish the memories of the Army Air Forces from my mind. The war was simply an experience of my past and there were few occasions to talk about it.

That has changed for several reasons. First, there's been a rebirth of interest in WW II with a new stream of books and movies aimed at an audience too young to remember that war. Second, a few years ago, I uncovered a box of my wartime letters to my parents and these loosened up my own data bank of memory. But mostly, I worried that the sweep of America's role in the most colossal war in history might someday be reduced, or even worse, forgotten by those who would come by later.

I'm grateful that my children have not had to bend their lives around a compulsory hitch in the armed services, to say nothing of actually going to war. I hope that no one's children will ever have to do the things that my generation did. I hope that the combat veterans alive today will be the last this country will ever see. As Chief Joseph, the American Indian leader once said, "We will fight no more forever." Amen!

In October of 1944, I composed the following poem after returning from a terrifying mission we had flown to Vienna. It is reproduced here exactly as I wrote it.

B-24 OVER VIENNA

'Tis night and you are dreaming, but the S-2 men are scheming,
    And you're sure to be awakened, 'ere dawn is in the sky.
Yes, a mission on the morrow, you'll learn to your great sorrow,
    We're bound for Hitler's fortress before the sun is high.

The C.Q. soon awakes you, his calloused hand it shakes you,
    In the bitter dawn you struggle with your kit.
You can swallow down some chow, but of course it's tasteless now,
    And you're off to briefing feeling far from fit.

Now in history it is told how the brave in times of old,
    Would hearten at the news of coming strife.
But the crews of twenty-fours, although hardened to the wars,
    Would tremble at the news of death or life.

For on life and death depend us on the target that they send us,
    The target's call informs us of our fate.
Yes, the mission's destination is a grim prognostication,
    And today Vienna's written on our slate.

Oh, Vienna land of art and of music near our heart,
    Home of sausage, wine, and dreamy Johann Strauss,
But your waltzes Viennese, will hardly us appease,
    For the flak comes up like thunder from your house.

While S-2's voice assures us, his proposal does unnerve us,
    And Vienna's flak cannot be put aside.
Then they give us all the poop that will soon effect our Group
    As each brass hat hands us ideas for our ride.

So we head down to the line with a chill inside our spine,
    In our mouths the taste recalling last nights beer.
We put on our heated suits and we tighten up our chutes,
    And we check Mae Wests and masks and other gear.

Five hundreds we will carry, delayed fuses which will bury,
    Demos deep into Vienna's Nazi hide.
Maximum gas goes in our tank and the ammo belts they clank,
    And the navigator's charts are stowed inside.

Now we climb into the ship and we taxi towards the strip,
    The crew chief's good luck shout is lost midst all the roar.
But he knows as sure as hell that it's best to wish us well,
    For we're cursed, we men who fly the twenty-four.

The pilot shoves the throttles full and the props begin to pull,
    But she takes her own sweet time to leave the ground.
For with thirty tons or more, she cannot really soar,
    And her engines scream a chill producing sound.

We've been airborne for a time and we're straining in a climb,
    When the oil begins to leak in number four.
But let the engine burn, we'll have no quick return,
    'Til we satisfy and please the gods of war.

We rendezvous as planned and we bid goodbye to land,
    As the Adriatic comes into our view.
The formation's finally set, but the box commanders sweat,
    And Able One keeps calling Baker Two.

The lead navigator's hoarse as he tries to hold his course,
    The pilot's arms are aching from the stick.
And the gunners at their stations curse their chosen occupations,
    And the bombardier has long since ceased to kick.

Yes it's 55 below and the cowling's caked with snow,
    The cold creeps into every shaking lad.
At four miles in the sky, without oxygen you'll die,
    But the irritating mask near drives you mad.

We fight to keep formation in spite of all temptation,
    For there may be fighters somewhere in the sky.
Though the headset cramps your ears, you try your best to hear,
    The warning, "Bandits at 10 o'clock and high."

The IP at last is near, we wake up the bombardier,
    He nods and puts his eye against the sight.
Then he sets his course and rate and he prays he's not too late,
    For an undercast is drifting from the right.

And as his crosshairs track, he switches on his rack,
    The target's just below, a railroad junction.
He opens up the bay and he hollers "Bombs away,"
    And he hopes to God there'll be no rack malfunction.

At last here comes the flak, there's no holding it back,
    They're throwing up everything they've got.
It's become so very thick, it's enough to make you sick,
    And although it's cold as hell, your skin gets hot.

Those little coal black puffs look innocent enough,
    Coming up from twenty-thousand feet below.
But as jagged steel does rip, gaping holes into your ship,
    You pray to Him above to let you go.

You were briefed to rally right, so the pilot racks it tight,
    And you look around and find you're all alone.
For your box was blown apart, and you're eating out your heart,
    Thinking of the guys who'll never more see home.

Flack knocked out Charlie Two, and Easy Five was through,
    When she got one right inside her bomb bay door.
And the rest are just as shot, the whole Group has lost a lot.
    The saying's true, "It never rains but that it pours."

Your hydraulic lines are gone, the fuel pump's no longer on,
    And you've had to feather engine number one.
The two superchargers blew, so you're pulling fifty-two,
    And the cables now are held with chewing gum.

So you start the long haul home, all over hell you roam,
    For the navigator's lost in undercast.
You're afraid you'll maybe ditch, and in this plane it's a bitch,
    For a twenty-four's first plunge is sure its last.

You finally sight your field, but the power that you wield,
    Is nil because you're sweating out your gas.
So you hit the runway good, and you've no hydraulic fluid,
    And you pile up on the hardstand with a crash.

You're home practically whole, you've bombed old Hitler's soul,
    But you take no joy in this most pleasing fact.
For you'll fly again tomorrow, and more trouble you will borrow,
    And for fifty missions you'll keep going back.

This then is the finish, but try not you to diminish,
    The spirit of the saga of the men who fly in war.
For some there's so much glory, but not those in this story,
    They're the losers of the Air Corps for they fly the 24.

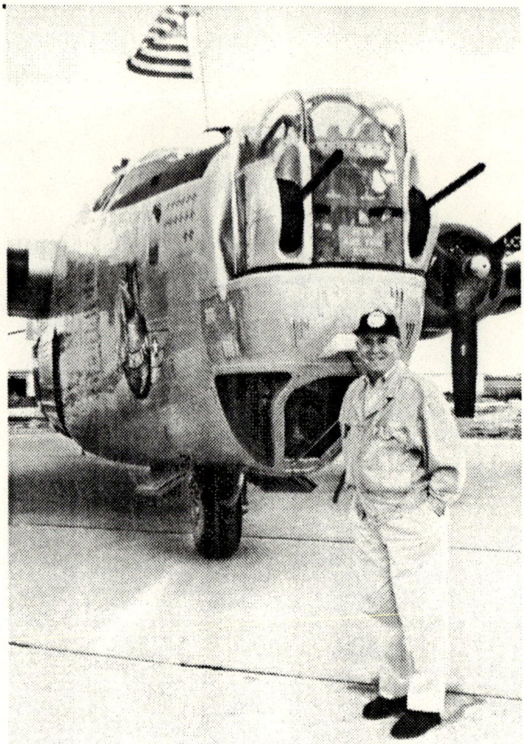